Praise for *Soul Dust*

"The great strength of this challenging and original foray into the 'hard question' of human consciousness is its combination of scientific rigor with exquisite sensitivity to the thoughts of philosophers, poets, religious thinkers, and humanists."

—Simon Blackburn, author of *Think: A Compelling Introduction to Philosophy*

"*Soul Dust*, Nicholas Humphrey's new book about consciousness, is seductive—early 1960s, 'Mad Men' seductive. His writing is as elegant, and hypnotic, as that cool jazz stacked on the record player. His argument feels as crystalline and bracing as that double martini going down."

—Alison Gopnik, *New York Times Book Review*

"Nicholas Humphrey begins where Crick and others have left off. He audaciously aims to provide a theoretical basis for understanding the level of consciousness that corresponds with one's personal qualitative experience. . . . Humphrey has laid out a new agenda for consciousness research."

—Michael Proulx, *Science*

"Humphrey offers an ingenious and crucial account of how it is that each of us experiences solely our own sensations, however much or little these echo what others report."

—*San Francisco Chronicle*

"[A] provocative book from a sparkling writer."

—Owen Flanagan, Duke University

NICHOLAS HUMPHREY

SOUL DUST

The Magic of Consciousness

PRINCETON UNIVERSITY PRESS

Princeton and Oxford

Published by Princeton University Press, 41 William Street,
Princeton, New Jersey 08540

In the United Kingdom: Princeton University Press, 6 Oxford Street,
Woodstock, Oxfordshire OX20 1TW

press.princeton.edu

Cover art: *Soul Dust 1*, 2010, acrylic ink. By Susan Aldworth. www.susanaldworth.com

Excerpt from *Yevtushenko: Selected Poems*, translated by Robin Milner-Gulland and
Peter Levi (Penguin Books, 1962). Copyright © Robin Milner-Gulland and Peter Levi,
1962. Reprinted by permission of Penguin Books Ltd.

Excerpt from "The Dog Beneath the Skin" by W. H. Auden, copyright © 1936, W. H.
Auden and Christopher Isherwood, reprinted by permission.

Excerpt from "Aubade" from *Collected Poems* by Philip Larkin, copyright © 1977, with
permission of Faber and Faber Ltd, publishers.

Fourth printing, and first paperback printing, 2013
Paperback ISBN 978-0-691-15637-8

The Library of Congress has cataloged the cloth edition of this book as follows
Humphrey, Nicholas.
    Soul dust : the magic of consciousness / Nicholas Humphrey.
        p.   cm.
    Includes bibliographical references and index.
    ISBN 978-0-691-13862-6 (hardcover : alk. paper)   1. Consciousness.   I. Title.
II. Title: Magic of consciousness.
    BF311.H7795 2011
    126—dc22   2010036759

This book has been composed in Garamond Premier Pro
Printed on acid-free paper. ∞
Printed in the United States of America

10 9 8 7 6 5 4

Truth is as impossible to be soiled by any outward touch

as the sunbeam; though this ill hap wait on her nativity,

that she never comes into the world, but like a bastard, to

the ignominy of him that brought her forth; till time, the

midwife rather than the mother of truth, have washed and

salted the infant [and] declared her legitimate.

—John Milton, *The Doctrine and Discipline of Divorce*, 1643

Contents

Contents
viii

 Invitation

I wrote a short book a few years ago—*Seeing Red: A Study in Consciousness*—that met with unexpectedly good reviews, even from my colleagues.[1] Unexpected, because the usual thing, in the field that has become known as "consciousness studies," is for academics to be dismissive of each other's ideas. The psychologist Walter Mischel has wryly noted: "Psychologists treat other people's theories like toothbrushes—no self-respecting person wants to use anyone else's."[2] Philosophers tend to be charier still.

The review that pleased me best was in the *American Journal of Psychology*: "This reviewer made at least three passes through the book, each pass yielding a new understanding. The first pass left me with a feeling of: 'Oh he doesn't really mean THAT!' But the second pass solidified and verified: 'Oh yeah he really does mean that.' And the third, and most rewarding pass: 'Oh my god, I think he's right!'"[3] Nonetheless, almost every discussion of *Seeing Red* had a sting in the tail. No one would allow that the problem of consciousness had actually been solved. Thus Steven Poole, writing in the *Guardian*: "But the 'hard problem' is still there, packed away into a corner of his argument. At some evolutionary stage, sensory feedback signals get 'privatised' in the brain and become 'about themselves.' Voilà, reflexivity and hence consciousness. But between stuff and thoughts there is still an argumentative crevasse. If there weren't, this would be an earth-shattering book. As it is, it is merely deeply interesting."[4]

They were right, of course; I had not solved the problem. Yet, who wants to have it said, as his epitaph, that his ideas were "merely deeply interesting"? I felt challenged to have one more go at writing the earth-shattering book—or, at any rate, the book that shows the fly the way out of the fly bottle.

This book, *Soul Dust,* takes off from the last few pages of *Seeing Red*. Since I cannot count on readers being familiar with my earlier work, I have reprised some of the ideas where needed. Apart from this, however, the arguments here are new. They are also, I must admit, largely untried by my peers. In this new book I have deliberately tried to change the game by following a different set of rules from those that have traditionally framed the discussion of consciousness. In doing this, and seeing for myself where it leads, I may say I have at times been surprised by the moves I have found myself making: "I can't really mean that. But yes I really do. In which case, here we go. . . ." In effect, the story has driven itself on. If the book reads—almost contrivedly—like a journey of discovery, that is because this is exactly what it has been in the writing.

My book is intended to be a work of serious science and philosophy, and I hope it will be judged as such. But it is also written for the general reader (while being furnished with copious scholarly notes). As it turns out, I could hardly have done otherwise than try to write a "popular book." For it becomes a central part of my argument that only by connecting to the interests and anxieties of conscious human beings in general can we begin to see the evolutionary raison d'être for the existence of consciousness in the first place. So, as the book proceeds to discuss the "whys" of consciousness, I come to focus, naturally, on issues having to do with life, death, and the meaning of existence—issues that matter so obviously to all ordinary human beings (even if they sometimes care about them more than they dare talk about them).

The result is that *Soul Dust,* which begins with the most basic questions about the nature of conscious awareness and sensation, becomes a book about the evolution of spirituality and how humans have made their home in what I call the "soul niche." Though I have no belief whatever in the supernatural, I make no apology for putting the human soul back where I am sure it belongs: at the center of consciousness studies.

Still, while the book does end up addressing many familiar human concerns, you should not expect it to be an easy read. There has been work to be done on my part, and it will require some work on yours. I begin the book by setting out my own account of what consciousness is and what the hard problem amounts to. This means my commencing with some relatively dry analysis and then, as the answers begin to emerge, some far-from-dry but still none-too-easy excursions into speculative neuroscience. At several points in part 1, I offer the reader a chance to skip to the next stage. But I hope in part 2, where I begin to ask what consciousness *is for*, the earlier work of establishing what it *is* starts to pay off. For if, as I argue, consciousness is no more or less than a piece of magical "theater," the questions about what it is for begin to look very different from those that philosophers and psychologists have been used to asking. And with very different questions come very different answers.

The answers I arrive at are certainly unlike any that science has yet had to offer. This in itself, I would have to agree, is no recommendation. Science is surely meant to be cumulative rather than revolutionary. Yet, when the fact is that previous research on consciousness has delivered almost nothing in the way of answers to the big questions people ask about the mystery of their experience, perhaps we can no longer rely on the science we are accustomed to.

The material world has given human beings magical souls. Human souls have returned the favor and put a magical spell upon the world. To understand these astonishing events, I invite you to start over.

PRELUDE

I   Coming-to Explained

Chances are it is less than a day since you regained consciousness. It probably happened soon after the sunlight returned this morning. What was it like for you, as you *came to*? Remember? The chink of a milk bottle, the touch of sheets, the sight of a patch of blue sky. You rubbed your eyes, stretched your limbs, and before you knew it, waves of *sensation* refilled the lake of your being. *You* re-emerged into the *subjective present*. Once more you *felt* yourself alive.

You were not alone. Something like this happened today to countless other individuals here on Planet Earth. Our planet, we are told, is merely a condensate of stardust, not so different from all the other minor cosmic bodies that litter the universe. But this one planet has become home to an extraordinary phenomenon. Here is where *sentience* evolved. Here is where *conscious selves* have come into their own. Here live *souls*.

In this book I will address the questions of what *sentience*, *selfhood*, and *soulfulness* amount to. In the course of it I will propose a solution to the "hard problem of consciousness." The hard problem is to explain how an entity made entirely of physical matter—such as a human being—can experience conscious feelings. The problem is *hard* because such feelings appear to us, who are the subjects of them, to have properties that could not possibly be conjured out of matter alone. We say—because we do not know what else to say—that "it's like something" to be conscious. Yet, the problem with this inadequate phrase, "it's like something," is that *what it is like* seems to us—no, *is* to us—unlike anything else out there in the material world.

There are philosophers who think the problem is simply too hard to admit of a solution. For Colin McGinn, trying to explain phenomenal consciousness as a product of the brain is like trying to explain how you can get "numbers from biscuits, or ethics from rhubarb."[1] For Jerry Fodor, "We can't, as things stand now, so much as imagine the solution of the hard problem. The revisions of our concepts and theories that imagining a solution will eventually require are likely to be very deep and very unsettling. . . . There is hardly anything that we may not have to cut loose from before the hard problem is through with us."[2]

I disagree. I acknowledge, of course, that theorists have not been doing too well in imagining the solution. I am as impressed as anyone by what *seem* to be the insuperable difficulties. But I suggest we attend to the word "seem." The fact that something *seems* to have mysterious and inexplicable features does not necessarily mean it really has them.

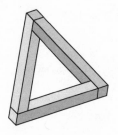

Figure 1.
The Penrose Triangle.

Let me illustrate the difference between *seeming impossible* and *being impossible* with the help of a well-known example. Suppose you were to come across a solid wooden object that looked just like the object shown in figure 1, Penrose's "impossible triangle." Certainly, it would seem to be a physical impossibility. Yet no one would say that just because of what the object *looks like* you should throw away your physics books and cut loose from everything you know. You would soon realize, of course, that it must be an illusion. And sure enough, if you could only *change your viewpoint,* you would discover that what you are actually looking at is the curious object shown on the next page in figure 2. This object was cunningly constructed by the psychologist Richard Gregory, precisely so that, when it is seen from a certain position, *it creates the impression* of an impossible triangle. This object deserves a name. With Gregory's permission, I call it the "Gregundrum."[3]

If you were to come across the Gregundrum lying on a laboratory bench, without knowing its "function," I am sure you would never guess that it holds the key to anything interesting. It is certainly not a pretty thing in its own right. Who would have thought that such a perfect thing as the Penrose triangle could have such an ugly explanation? Yet, as Sherlock Holmes said to Dr. Watson, "When you have eliminated the

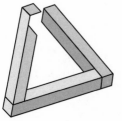

Figure 2.
The Gregundrum.

impossible, whatever remains, however improbable, must be the truth."[4]

I will argue that the truth about consciousness—if and when we see it from the right perspective—is that it is indeed the product of a highly improbable bit of biological engineering: a wonderful artwork of nature that gives rise to all sorts of mysterious impressions in our minds, yet something that has a relatively straightforward physical explanation. As Holmes went on, "We know that he did not come through the door, the window, or the chimney. We also know that he could not have been concealed in the room, as there is no concealment possible. Whence, then, did he come?" "He came through the hole in the roof," Watson cried. Our job as consciousness researchers is to find the hole in the roof.

I do not say it will be easy. To start with, in an area where theorists continually talk past each other, there will be issues about the use of *words*. To forestall at least some potential verbal misunderstandings, I have set out in the box a rough guide to the conceptual territory as I see it. (You should not get hung up on anything in this list at this stage—I will justify and explain these definitions further as we go on.)

But it is not just words that may come between us and the truth; it may be the deep-seated biases that we bring to the table as subjects of consciousness ourselves. We cannot of course

- In general, when I talk about consciousness I mean "phenomenal consciousness."

- A subject is "phenomenally conscious" (or plain "conscious") when and if there is something *it's like to be him* at this moment.

- There is "something it's like to be him" when he experiences *feelings*, or what philosophers call *qualia*.

- Qualia—for example, the felt redness of fire, the sweetness of honey, the pain of a bee sting—are features of *sensations*.

- The subject is "phenomenally conscious" just when he experiences sensations *as having* these peculiar features.

- To experience sensations "as having" these features is to form *a mental representation* to that effect (with the meaning of "represent" still to be decided).

- Thus "consciousness" (or "being conscious"), as a state of mind, is the *cognitive* state of entertaining such mental representations.

- Consciousness can change the subject's life just to the extent that these representations *feed forward to influence what he thinks and does*.

opt out of our privileged position, but we can at least try to imagine where we would be without it. To that end, I want to begin our investigation of the problem by handing it over to someone else, someone who should have a remoter and more objective view of what consciousness is doing for us than we ourselves have.

Coming-to Explained

■ Let us return, then, to this morning. Only now imagine that a few hundred miles out in space, a visiting scientist from an advanced civilization in the Andromeda galaxy is orbiting our planet, on her first trip to investigate life on Earth. (I call her "her" because I assume the Andromedans long ago dispensed with the male sex.)

Situating her craft so as to get a good view of the boundary as night turns to day on the Earth's surface, she observes how, all along this boundary, living creatures are emerging from their nighttime coma. Birds are breaking into song, butterflies are taking to the wing, monkeys are leaving their beds in the trees, and human beings are going downstairs to brew their morning coffee.

She observes this great awakening, and she nods knowingly. She recognizes, of course, that the central processors that run these earthlings' onboard software have been in sleep mode overnight, so as to save energy and perform system maintenance. And now, with the sun's rays bringing light and warmth, it is time for them to resume their life tasks. As a scientist, she has much to look forward to. Once she gets down among these creatures, how interesting it will be for her to study their brains and behavior and figure out how it all works. Indeed, she fancies herself as a bit of a philosopher: one day she will write a book called *Coming-to Explained*.

Our visitor has every reason to trust the scientific method. Wherever else in the universe she and her colleagues have applied it, natural phenomena have given up their secrets. No doubt, she reckons, there can be nothing so different or difficult about those living organisms down there on Earth.

But is she right? What about *consciousness*? Will it ever dawn on the Andromedan visitor that there is a dimension to the lives of at least some of the creatures she is studying that needs special treatment, that when they "come to," it is as if a light is coming on *inside* their heads? Given that she can see things only from outside, is it possible that she will miss this altogether, that she will never even suspect that consciousness exists?[5]

▪ I think we should assume the Andromedan does not have the circuits in her own brain that would make her phenomenally conscious herself. Otherwise we will not know how to assess any claims she may make to have *discovered* the existence of consciousness in other creatures. (She might just be arguing from analogy with her own case, in the way you or I might argue, for example, that it is obvious that a dog feels pain the way we do.)

The absence of phenomenal consciousness may or may not affect the way she thinks about philosophical and scientific issues (this is something we should be better placed to judge by the end of the book). But I see no reason, as of now, why it should place any limit on her intelligence ("artificial intelligence," as we might want to call it) or her skills at scientific research. Let us suppose, indeed, that she does have an exceptionally brilliant analytic mind. And let us allow her every other scientific advantage anyone might ask for. She can undertake meticulous behavioral studies of how earthlings behave in the wild, and then follow up this fieldwork with whatever laboratory investigations are suggested. She has all the research instruments she could possibly need: scanners and imagers and calculators of a sophistication yet undreamed of here on Earth. She can prod and probe and listen in and cross-question. She can, if she wants, take the earthlings apart and examine their machinery (the Andromedan ethics committees have no objection to alien vivisection). Then, back home, she will be able to run theoretical simulations on her computer and build working models in the robot shop.

Then, what *will* she discover, and what will she not? Let us consider some possibilities.

- She will find, to her surprise, that in order to explain the *behavior* of certain species of earthlings, she needs to postulate the existence of an extraspecial mental state—a state with peculiar qualitative properties, unlike anything else, which *just because of what it is like* is changing how these creatures live their lives.
- Though perhaps she will be unable to deduce the existence of any such special inner state from what she observes of public behavior, she will nevertheless realize that such a state exists when she examines in detail the flow of information in the earthlings' brains and figures out what kind of *private mental representations* are being generated.
- She will do better still. Beyond simply discovering the existence of conscious states, she will be able—either from behavioral observations or from brain scans—to arrive at a complete description of what it is like to be the subject of a particular state. Perhaps she will even get to the point where she can compare one individual's state with another's—so that she can tell, for example, whether different subjects are experiencing the sensation of red in the same way.
- Or then again, perhaps she will be able to do none of the above.

Now, as it happens, there are a good many students of consciousness here on Earth—they may even be in the majority—who believe the answer can be only the last of these. In their view our visitor will fail to discover *anything* about consciousness by any of the scientific means at her disposal because of an awkward but undeniable truth: consciousness, for all its subjective importance, *is physically featureless; it does not show.*

The psychologist Jeffrey Gray has written, for example, "Nothing that we so far know about behaviour, physiology, the evolution of either behaviour or physiology, or the possibilities of constructing automata to carry out complex forms of behaviour, is such that the hypothesis of consciousness would arise, if it did not occur in addition as a datum in our own experience; nor, having arisen, does it provide a useful explanation of the phenomena observed in those domains."[6]

Others have gone further still, arguing for what the philosopher Owen Flanagan has called "consciousness inessentialism"—"the view that for any intelligent activity *I*, performed in any cognitive domain *d*, even if *we* do *I* with conscious accompaniments, *I* can in principle be done without these conscious accompaniments."[7] Thus, according to John Searle, "We could have *identical behavior* in two different systems, one of which is conscious and the other totally unconscious."[8] There could even exist a "philosophical zombie human," David Chalmers has suggested, who is physically identical to a normal human being and who looks and acts in every respect just like one, yet who is not phenomenally conscious—"all is dark inside."[9] Then, if you or I were to meet such a philosophical zombie in the street, we would not—and could not—know the difference.

True, each of us is presumably convinced that consciousness exists in our own case, and therefore we may want to give the benefit of the doubt to others who so obviously resemble us. But the Andromedan scientist does *not* know about consciousness from her own case. Therefore, if and when *she* notes resemblances between herself and any of the earthling creatures she is studying (those naked bipeds who seem to have taken over the planet are certainly technologically ingenious!), she is likely to assume they resemble her in this respect as well. And if consciousness inessentialism is right, she will not discover anything in the course of her research to make her revise her opinion. At the end of the day, she will not think she has missed anything. So she will return to Andromeda—and write her book—with a satisfied sense of mission accomplished: "Coming-to Explained Away."

I said I wanted to hand over the investigation of the hard problem to this visitor, because we might expect her to have "a remoter and more objective view of what consciousness is doing for us than we ourselves have." But if this is really how things stand, it seems the problem will not even cross her horizon. Fodor wrote, "There is hardly anything that we may not have to cut loose from before the hard problem is through with us." He cannot have meant this interpretation, but is the lesson that if we want to keep up with the best science in the universe, we ought to cut loose from the concept of consciousness itself?

▓ You will realize—if for no other reason than because my own book does not end here—that I do not think so. My starting point is that consciousness, however elusive and enigmatic from a scientific perspective, is a fact of nature. And if it is not *evidently* a fact of nature, that can be only because scientists and philosophers have been looking for evidence in the wrong places. I believe this because I think the idea that consciousness has no observable effects is daft (and the notion of a "philosophical zombie"—a physical duplicate of a conscious human who completely lacks consciousness—is dafter still). However, I have to say I do not think it is daft to suppose that certain aspects of conscious experience could have no observable effects. So, before we go further, I want to consider just to what extent conscious experience will—and will not—be observable to an outsider.

We know, of course, that not everything that goes on in the mind of a person or an animal has to show up *in behavior*. There can obviously be purely private mental states. Indeed, most ordinary mental states are private, insofar as they occur without anyone's—except the subject—knowing about them. No one but you knows what your thoughts are right now (why else would anyone give you a penny for them?). No one but me knows about my dreams last night (and, as it happens, even I do not know any longer).

Still, we might want to argue that states such as these are only contingently private. If you were given the penny, you *could* tell me what your thoughts are. If I had kept a dream diary, I *could* have shared my dream with you. And even without language, there would probably be ways of communicating much of the content of these mental states.

But that is *thoughts*. And with *feelings* it would seem to be a different matter. How about basic sensory experiences? They undoubtedly seem to be more absolutely private. You would be hard put to it, however much you tried, to reveal the full content of what it is like to experience the smell of a rose or

Coming-to Explained

the coldness of a snowball. Though you could surely communicate some part of it, you would not know how to capture the subjective quality of the sensations, the qualia.

It is by no mean obvious exactly what the problem is. Is it that there is something about the logical status of qualia, as intrinsically subjective properties, that makes them incommunicable in principle? Or is it simply that in practice we do not have the requisite communication skills? Could it even be that our minds have been designed to have some kind of fire wall around sensory experience which puts adaptive limits on what others can discover about us?

There could be some truth in all these possibilities. But whatever is causing the problem, we must surely accept that there *is* a problem; we must concede that in practice, even if not in principle, conscious sensations are private in crucial respects, so that nothing the subject can say or do can reveal everything about them.

However, I would say this is *all* we need concede. We need not—and should not—accept either of two stronger propositions, namely, (1) while an outside observer is restricted to studying behavior, she will not even be able to detect that phenomenal consciousness *is present*, and (2) even if the observer were allowed complete access to the subject's brain, she would not be able to discover *the full content*.

Let us look at these two issues. First, why do I believe that consciousness must reveal its *presence*, if nothing more, at the level of behavior?

The reason is the ultimate one, the hand of natural selection. Since consciousness, as we know it, is a feature of life on earth, we can take it for granted that—like every other specialized feature of living organisms—it has evolved because it confers selective advantage. In one way or another, it must be helping the organism to survive and reproduce. And of course this can happen only if somehow it is changing the way the organism *relates to the outside world.*

Now, how could this be happening? Conscious creatures do not smell different or look prettier. Consciousness does not provide extra strength or better health. Instead, consciousness can have its effects on survival only by changing what we may loosely call the creature's "psychology." In other words, being phenomenally conscious must be influencing how the creature *thinks* or what it *wants* or what it *believes*, in just such a way that it now acts in the world in adaptive ways it would not have done otherwise.

In later chapters I will explore in detail just how this may be working: how the effects may be present on several levels, and how they may be more or less important for different kinds of animals, pushing the evolution of consciousness along species-specific lines. As we will see, human beings, with their developed sense of "conscious self," are most likely in a class of their own. But the important point for now is that if natural selection can "see" the effects—whatever they are—of the changed psychology on behavior, presumably so too can other outside observers (if only they knew where to look). What is more, if these observers can see what natural selection sees, they should also be able to see what it is about it that is beneficial—and hence why natural selection has favored it. Thus they should be well on their way to constructing a story about *why* consciousness evolved.

Still, do not get me wrong about this. I am not suggesting that because consciousness has been designed by natural selection, this means that every one of the features of the design must be able to be seen from the outside. Rather, what it means is that every one of these features must be contributing to the beneficial effects that natural selection *does* see.

It would be easy to misunderstand this, so let me tell a parable to make it clearer. Imagine that in a certain country the government has a Department of Happiness, whose minister has the job of maximizing the general happiness of the population. The minister must therefore be on the lookout for things that put people into a good humor. One day he comes across a group of people who are looking at a cartoon and smiling broadly. From where he stands, the minister cannot actually see the picture they are looking at, and so he does not get the joke. Still, he can see the positive feelings the cartoon is eliciting. And that is enough to persuade him to take departmental action to "breed" this cartoon by ordering additional cartoons in the same style. So he does this, and the next day he sees more people laughing at the new drawings. He repeats his order, and soon enough cartoons in this special style are everywhere. The style has become, as it were, a ministerial design feature. But note that at no point has the minister himself needed to know what the cartoons look like. All he has needed to see is evidence that the cartoons exist and that they are funny.

My point is that, likewise, natural selection need never have known what conscious experience is actually like for the subject. All it must have seen is evidence that conscious experience exists and that it is in some way life enhancing. This being the case, it is possible and even quite likely that the detailed phenomenal content of sensations will not ever have been evident in behavior. And so today our visiting scientist, while she relies on outside observations, will be able to get only halfway to discovering the facts of consciousness. She should certainly be able to detect that the special inner state exists in some creatures and that, in whatever way their behavior suggests, it adds to their success in life. However, this may well be as far as she can go.[10]

▪ Yet, what if she were able to *search inside their heads*? Why do I believe that an observer who can go beyond behavior down to the level of brain activity should be able to discover *all* there is to know?

My reason is simply the guiding principle, which underlies all science, that *nothing interesting occurs without a material cause*. In short, *miracles do not happen*. When conscious experience arises in a person's mind, it is the outcome of events in the brain. Moreover, if and when these events (in their totality) occur, the outcome *has to be* that the person is conscious (which is why the idea of a philosophical zombie makes no sense). Thus, if a scientist can go inside and observe these crucial events, she should be able, in principle, to deduce what the outcome is—provided only that she has a *theory* linking brain states to experience, a theory that enables her to move from one level of description to the other.

What kind of theory would this be? Philosopher Dan Lloyd has written: "What we need is a transparent theory. One that, once you get it, you see that anything built like *this* will have *this* particular conscious experience."[11] We can draw an analogy with explaining the properties of water. Scientists are able to deduce that a pail of molecules, whose chemical composition is H_2O, at room temperature will have the physical properties of the substance we know as water (fluidity, wetness, and so on) because, with their understanding of the laws of physical chemistry, they have a theory of why *water under its chemical description* must amount to *water under its physical description.*

Then, so too, we may reasonably hope that if and when scientists have a comparable understanding of the laws of what we may call neurophenomenology, so that they have a theory of why *brain activity under its neuroscientific description* must amount to *mental activity under its experiential description,* they will be able to deduce that, for example, a man whose brain is in a particular state is a man who is thinking such and such thoughts.[12]

It is already widely agreed by those who study mind-brain relationships that it is the pattern of information flow in the brain that determines mental states. I would say we can assume therefore that the neurophenomenological laws will essentially be laws about *how experience is computed.* Admittedly, apart from having this one insight, our scientists here on Earth are nowhere near to discovering what the laws actually are. Still, we need not doubt that the laws exist and will eventually be found out. So, to continue with our story of the Andromedan scientist, let us imagine that the theorists on Andromeda are far more advanced than ours are, and—in anticipation of their sister's mission (or perhaps just for the fun of it)—they have worked out ahead of time the relevant laws as they apply to alien brains.

Thus, let us suppose the Andromedan scientist has arrived among us prearmed with the theoretical tools she needs for interpreting earthlings' brain activity in experiential terms. Where will this take her? Given what was said above, we may assume that, on the basis of her purely behavioral observations, she will already have concluded that in some of the earthlings under study (notably, human beings) there does exist a special inner state that is influencing their outlook on life—though a state of which the detailed content is so far a mystery to her. But now that her brain research is under way, she will, with the help of the theory, be able to deduce that these particular subjects are having experiences with exactly the weird and wonderful phenomenal content that you and I know so well firsthand.

"Well, blow me!" she may say. "Who'd have guessed it?" For she will indeed have deduced the existence of qualia. She will, as it were, have arrived at a complete description of the private joke that lies behind the public smile.

Are you with me still? Or do you think I have tried to pull a fast one on you (in fact, did I not try to pull it a few pages back)? Can it be true that the Andromedan—who is not conscious herself, remember—has discovered what consciousness is *really* like? Or has she merely discovered its pale shadow?

The big question, you may insist, is whether the scientist, when she examines the brain of someone who is having a conscious sensation, can deduce what that person's experience *actually is,* and not merely deduce a *description of what that experience is* (and calling it a "phenomenological description" simply begs the question).

But, no, I have not pulled a fast one. Rather, if you make this objection, I would say you have just pulled a fast one on yourself. You have fallen for the tempting idea that there is something conscious experience *actually is* that is separate from what the subject *thinks* it is—that is, the *mental representation* that he makes of it. But it is not so. If you do not see

Coming-to Explained

19

this now, I hope to persuade you of it as we go on. To give a foretaste of what is coming, in the very next chapter I will argue that what I called at the start of this book the inadequate phrase "it's like something" is not such a bad phrase after all. Because, when it comes to it, for a subject to have a sensory experience that *is like something* really is for him to represent the object of experience *as if it is something* with some very peculiar features. In short, for the subject to have a sensory experience that is like something is just for him to experience it *as what it is like.*

The philosopher John Searle (with whom, on the question of consciousness, I agree about very little) put his finger on this point precisely when he wrote: "If it seems to me exactly as if I am having conscious experiences, then I am having conscious experiences."[13] Just so. "Seems to Searle exactly as if" can only mean "is represented mentally by Searle exactly as being."

What follows from this? Since mental representations can, in principle, always be described or re-represented in some public medium—they would not count as representations otherwise—it surely follows that, despite what was said above about the de facto incommunicability of private experience, it must be possible in principle to *describe* what it is like to be conscious.

It is undeniably true that, as of now, we humans do not know how to do this satisfactorily. We lack both the theory and the language for the job. But these, we should assume, are contingent limitations—already overcome in Andromeda and soon enough to be overcome back here on Earth.

I would say we should acknowledge that the phenomenological descriptions of conscious experience that will feature in the final theory will probably require a new vocabulary, even a new grammar.[14] But we should not be too alarmed by this, let alone see it as a reason for giving up. It has happened before in the history of science that scientists required a new conceptual language before they could move on—and yet, after initial awkwardness and even disbelief, soon enough everyone gets used to it. Think, for example, of how mathematics has had to come to terms with "complex numbers" involving the square root of minus one, or of "transfinite numbers" that are bigger than infinity. Think of how physics has had to come to terms with relativity.

Future descriptions of conscious experience will almost certainly require concepts that sit oddly with our standard ways of thinking today. I already remarked at the opening of this chapter that the problem with saying "it is like something" to be conscious is that *what it is like* seems to us—no, *is* to us—unlike anything else out there in the material world. The phenomenal experience of the "subjective present" as existing in "thick time"—as I have attempted to describe it elsewhere[15] and as I will revisit shortly—is perhaps just such an apparently *essential* yet *nonsensical* concept.

Yet, let us stick with our story. We have assumed that scientists on Andromeda are well ahead of us in recognizing the neurophenomenological laws. Contained within this assumption must be the assumption that they have already developed a suitably esoteric language for describing conscious experience (even if the development of this language must have been, as it were, "on spec," since the Andromedans, having never encountered creatures such as human beings before, cannot yet have had occasion to apply it).[16] So we are assuming that our visitor will have the tools for describing what it is like for us, even if we humans at present do not.

Coming-to Explained

However, I do not want to make our own inadequacy an absolute sticking point. To claim—as many philosophers would—that consciousness is *essentially ineffable* is to underestimate human ingenuity and creativity. As we will see later in this book, humans may be more capable of expressing publicly what it is like to be conscious than the philosophical and scientific skeptics would have us believe—though when they do so, they "cheat" by using the language of *art* rather than that of *science*. Well, we will see.[17]

■ This introductory chapter, which started off so breezily, is getting heavy. It is time to sum up—and lighten up, if possible.

I wanted the Andromedan scientist's help with the project of understanding the hard problem—the nature of consciousness—because I hoped that to see the problem from her perspective might provide us with some useful guidelines for our own inquiry. Whatever the differences between us and her are, I take it that *science is science* wherever in the universe it is being done. What counts as evidence and conclusions for this researcher from a far-off galaxy should be what counts as such for us on Earth. That is why I asked above what will the Andromedan find out about consciousness, and what will she not. I assume this is what, at the limits of our human abilities, we can expect to find out too.

Here is the score.

We have established that the Andromedan scientist will be able to discover at a behavioral level crucial hints that consciousness is present in some creatures. At the very least, she will discover that consciousness is having certain beneficial effects—these are the effects on which natural selection has been acting in the course of evolution. She will discover that consciousness *exists* and—in the larger picture—what consciousness *is for*.

Nevertheless, while she stays on the outside, she will probably be unable to reach a deep understanding of the contents of consciousness. This is because the crucial features of what it is like for the subject will, in normal circumstances, probably be hidden from public view—even though these features are ultimately responsible for the beneficial effects.

To find out more of the details, she will have to go inside. When she does so, using all the neuroscientific techniques at her disposal, she should indeed be able to discover *everything* about what it is like to be conscious, provided she has a *theory*. But this neurophenomenological theory will have to be a new and remarkable theory: not a theory that we human beings can never get to understand (as some philosophers, notably Colin McGinn, have suggested),[18] but certainly a theory we will not understand until we have put in some more work.

So now, let me set out my agenda for this work and my book. What I plan to do is to emulate, in my own way, the Andromedan scientist's investigation. Yet, because, first, I am not as clever as she is, and, second, I am a living example of the phenomenon under investigation, my strategic goals will be a little different.

On Andromeda, I have suggested, scientists have already developed the theoretical tools for solving the hard problem of how matter could in principle give rise to consciousness, even if they have never yet come across a case of consciousness in fact. By contrast, we humans know consciousness exists in fact, but we do not at the moment have the theory of it. The first task for the book, then, must be to come up with at least the beginnings of a plausible theory of what consciousness *is* and how it relates to the brain. To do this I will, in the next few chapters, argue for a radically new account of what we mean when we say that "it is like something" to experience sensations. I will make a proposal as to what *the thing in the brain* that the subject represents as "being like something" really is, and I will suggest what its biological origins in nonconscious animals may have been.

The Andromedan scientist, I have assumed, being completely new to the world of conscious creatures, will, at the start, have no idea what difference consciousness is making at either the private or the public level, let alone what good, if any, comes of it. By contrast, we humans know rather a lot about the difference that consciousness is making to our private lives, though we are far from understanding how this translates into public benefits. The second task for the book then will be to figure out—knowing what we already do—how being conscious changes people's psychology (and perhaps that of other conscious animals as well) in ways that ultimately increase their chances of survival.

Having read this far, you may be nervous that the book is going to be unduly scientistic. Do not worry. There is indeed work to be done. We need to get the science right if we can. But my book is called *Soul Dust,* and it will live up to that title. The book will continue with some hard-going philosophical analysis, but it will end with a fairy tale—a scientifically based fairy tale—about how consciousness lights up the world.

PART ONE

2   Being "Like Something"

So we want a theory of what being conscious is like and how this could result from the activity of nerve cells in the brain. If only it did not make us feel so queasy just to think about it! Four hundred years ago René Descartes described his own plight as a human mind trying to think about the nature of its own experience: "It feels as if I have fallen unexpectedly into a deep whirlpool which tumbles me around so that I can neither stand on the bottom nor swim up to the top."[1]

We need something to help us get our bearings. Some clever new idea. Yet where to look for it? If I say I want to start with the *language* people use, you may be disappointed. Surely, you may think, philosophers in the last century pretty well exhausted that approach without solving any important scientific problems. Maybe it is true that Ludwig Wittgenstein, in his *Philosophical Investigations,* helped clear the air around consciousness by showing how the ways people talk about mental states can lead them astray, creating conundrums and mysteries that do not really exist. But did not Wittgenstein's analysis prove signally unhelpful to understanding what *does exist*?

Yes, it did. However, that was then. And the zeitgeist of consciousness studies is very different fifty years later. The identification of the problem of qualia as the "hard problem" has changed what questions are worth asking.[2] When the price of gold goes up, it can be worth reopening seams that were supposedly mined out long ago.

■ "*It is like something.*" I do not know when people—at least those writing in English—first started to use this phrase to refer to the essence of being conscious. But the use was already well established when Tom Nagel, in 1974, wrote his famous essay "What Is It Like to Be a Bat?" In that essay Nagel simply asserted (rather as I did in the previous chapter) that *being like something* is the defining property of consciousness: "Fundamentally an organism has conscious mental states if and only if there is something that it is like to *be* that organism—something it is like *for* the organism."[3] He took it for granted that his readers would understand what he was referring to. And so it seems they did. The fact that this way of talking has subsequently become widespread in both philosophical and popular writing suggests that it must somehow sit peculiarly well with people's first-person understanding of what being conscious means.

Why ever should this be? Since words gain their meaning from how they are used across the language, presumably the use of "it is like something" in relation to consciousness must have something in common with its use in other contexts. So, can we look to ordinary English for a clue?

Now, in pretty much every other situation, when we say "X is like Y" (for example, "This wine is like a Beaujolais"), what we mean is that in our view X *resembles* Y or X *shares some salient property* with Y. However, we mean something rather more than this too. Note that we would never say "X is like Y" when we know that X actually *is* Y. So when we say "X is like Y," we mean X shares some particular property with Y, but—so far as we know at this time—*it does not share all its other properties*. True, sometimes we may want to imply that since it shares at least this particular property, X *could* share all of its other properties with Y. But there has to be at the least some uncertainty about it. It has to be unconfirmed whether X is Y in fact. "This wine is like a Beaujolais, it could even *be* a Beaujolais, though I'm not sure it is not actually a Chianti."

Suppose, then, that when we say "it is like something for someone to experience a sensation," we mean the subject is literally *likening* his sensation to something in just this sense. What might this tell us about consciousness?

I proposed already in the previous chapter that for someone to be conscious of having a sensation must involve his representing the object of experience *as* something with properties of a special and peculiar kind. But now this would be taking matters considerably further. It would be suggesting that for someone to be conscious of having the sensation involves his representing the object of experience *as if it is something that it may not be*—something he has certainly not been able to confirm it is.

Let us suppose the someone in question is you.[4] Then, when you say "it is like something for me to see red," for example, you would be implying that, strictly speaking, your sensation is a hypothetical entity. Indeed, if we were to follow this line, I would go beyond this: I think you would be implying that the sensation is *intrinsically* hypothetical, for the phenomenology suggests that the as-if, unconfirmed quality of the representation is not just a temporary or remediable condition. When you say it is like something to see red, you are not allowing that soon enough you may discover the truth about whether the sensation actually is this something. You would never expect to say: "I thought the red sensation merely resembled this, but then I found out it actually was this."

No. Sensations, it would seem, are *always as-if*. So, in this regard, the being-like-something of sensations is different from the being-like-something of the wine. With the wine, if you say "it is like a Beaujolais," you are assuming there is a discoverable fact of the matter as to whether it actually is a Beaujolais or a Chianti. With sensations, however, if you say "it is like something for me to see red," you are assuming no such thing: whatever the fact of the matter about the red sensation, it is not discoverable by you as the subject—nothing could help you to decide once and for all whether *what it is like* is *what it is*.

But this is remarkable. What can be going on, such that it would make sense to say of X that it resembles Y, even though you could never in principle have the evidence to alter your opinion about whether X actually is Y?

There is only one set of circumstances I can think of where this might be appropriate: it would be when you recognize that Y does not or could not exist as an entity belonging to the ordinary world where you can test things, but might exist in another world with different rules to which you have no direct access—indeed, where *X is evidence of there being such another world*.

Imagine, by analogy, that you are facing a wall on which the shadows of solid objects passing behind you are being cast by the light of a blazing fire some distance farther back. What do these shadows look like to you? "This shadow is like a cart." "This one is like a bird." But you cannot confirm that the objects are what their shadows resemble because you cannot turn around and enter directly into their three-dimensional world.

I have taken you now—you may be as surprised as I am—to Plato's famous story of the cave. In *The Republic* Plato uses this analogy to explain how there might exist a world of transcendental entities—"pure forms" or "substances"—of which human beings have only indirect and partial knowledge. I did not expect our discussion to lead so soon to Plato's metaphysics. But now that it has, let me cite a revealing remark by the painter Bridget Riley. Writing about visual sensations, she says: "For all of us, colour is experienced *as something*—that is to say, we always see it *in the guise of a substance*."[5] Does her choice of that word, "substance," suggest she believes that we do indeed liken sensation to something belonging to a higher level of reality? *The phenomenal is transcendental?* Is *that* what we imply by using the language of "it's like"?

Well, maybe, kind of. I hope all will become clearer in due course. But now let us explore this idea further, without asking for too much clarity at the beginning. Suppose it were so; what kind of transcendental/phenomenal world might we be talking about? With the analogy of the cave leading us on, let

Being "Like Something"

me suggest, to start with, that this would have to be a world that requires at least one novel extra dimension to describe it (whether a physical or a conceptual dimension, we will see). And yet what would be the status of such a world? Would it have to exist for real?

I am sure that for most people "consciousness realism" is irresistible. Sensations undoubtedly exist, and sensations are like entities in the phenomenal world. So presumably the phenomenal world must have a substantive existence. But even though this may be how most laypeople see it, it is another question entirely whether theoreticians should see it this way too. Since things in this other world apparently have such exotic properties, and since their existence cannot be independently confirmed, surely we ought to consider seriously the possibility that it is some kind of make-believe—not real at all but an *illusion*. That is, sensation might be merely *appearing*, as Riley so well put it, *in the guise* of a substance.

Yet this would point to further remarkable goings-on. If the phenomenal properties of sensation are an illusion, this can hardly be just a stroke of good luck. Conscious experience is altogether too impressive—even too perfect—to have been thrown together by chance. There would obviously have had to be some method behind it. In short, the evidence that leads you to believe in the existence of phenomenal entities would have had to be *planted*. We would be dealing, as it were, with a *coup de théâtre*.

Let us pause for breath and collect these thoughts. From examining the phrase "it is like something to be conscious," we have now raised an extraordinary possibility, or rather two. First, from the subject's point of view, consciousness appears

Chapter 2

to be a gateway to a transcendental world of as-if entities. Second, from the point of view of theory, consciousness is the product of some kind of illusion chamber, a charade.

Is this the clever new idea we need? Consciousness as a Platonic shadow play performed in an internal theater, to impress the soul! It would certainly take us into interesting new territory. It might even explain why the hard problem sometimes seems not just intractable but so *gloriously* intractable.

The philosopher Natika Newton has remarked, "Phenomenal consciousness itself is *sui generis*. Nothing else is like it *in any way at all*."[6] The Koran says of Allah, "[Allah is] the originator of the heavens and the earth . . . [there is] nothing like a likeness of Him."[7] When the going gets mysterious, mysteries get going. Suddenly the quasi-magical properties of qualia would no longer pose such a problem.[8] Magic is just what is to be expected in a magic show.

But that is for later. I would say the immediate reason to be pleased with this idea as the basis for a scientific theory of consciousness is that it allows us to start thinking about the brain basis of it all. If sensations were truly to have out-of-this-world properties, there is no question that the search for a theory would be in trouble. However, it is an entirely different story if sensations merely have *as-if* out-of-this-world properties.

Let us exchange Plato's cave for a more humdrum analogy. I want to return to the model that you may have realized I have had in mind since early on: the "real impossible triangle" with which I opened the previous chapter. It is becoming clearer where to steer the line of thought.

Suppose, once more, you were to be confronted by the wooden object, the Gregundrum, as shown next in figure 3.

Figure 3.

Now, however, for the sake of argument, I want to place you squarely in the special position of Observer A in this diagram, the one position from which it appears that the top arms of the triangle are coincident so that you see the whole thing as joined up.

As we noted earlier, if only you could move to the position of Observer B, you would see things differently. But this time, let us suppose, so as to give you a truly special perspective on it, that things are rigged so that, as and when you move around the object, some hidden hand turns it so that it is always facing you in the same way. (Compare how it is to look in a mirror and to find your eyes always looking straight back at you.)

Then, what does the object look like to you? You see it presumably as an impossible object. You represent it in your mind as such. If asked to explain what you are perceiving to other people, you might very well prefer to define it ostensively by inviting them to come and see it for themselves from your position. However, assuming there is no opportunity for them to do this, I expect you could, if pressed, *tell* them about it in words—that is, you could describe the perceived object as it does indeed appear to you.

Here, I will do it for you (refer back, if you like, to the larger illustration of figure 1). "What I see is an unbroken solid triangular object, made of three square-cross-section posts of equal length. The posts are connected at right angles, so that, starting at the bottom left corner, the arm to the right is angled away from me at 45 degrees; at the right corner the arm to the left is angled away at 45 degrees; at the top corner the arm downward is angled away at 45 degrees."

The description is surely accurate so far. This is indeed what you perceive the object to be in terms of its elements. Yet, even as you perceive it as being this, you are well aware that such a triangle as a whole could not possibly exist in the ordinary world. So, I would guess you will want to add: "What I see is either (a) evidence of there being a world to which the rules of physics do not apply or (b) some kind of trick." However, since no one in his right mind would posit the existence of a nonphysical world merely because he is confronted by a wooden object that he cannot explain, "everything considered, this has to be a trick."[9]

So, how does this bear on the mystery of sensations and qualia? What I suggest is that the logic of the situation you find yourself in when you have a sensation is very much the same as when you are confronted by the Gregundrum—although the psychological impact is different in two crucial respects.

You look at a ripe tomato, for example, and in response to the red light reaching your eyes, something happens in your brain that you experience as the sensation of red. We can say that, like Observer A, you clearly have a special perspective on this brain activity. It is only from your privileged position as the subject of the experience that the brain activity does indeed come across as a conscious sensation. An outside observer, if she could observe this same brain activity, would be like Observer B and never get it.

Then, what does the sensation *feel like* to *you*? You experience it as having the phenomenal quality of "red," which, strange to say, is somehow *out of this world*. Again you represent it in your mind *as* such. If asked to explain to others, your first thought, as with the triangle, will be to invite them to share the wonder of it by experiencing it for themselves. However, if there is no opportunity for them to do this, it is now a different story from the triangle, because you will not find it straightforward to describe it. In fact, you may find yourself completely tongue-tied.

So here is the first difference. The phenomenal qualities of sensations are next to impossible to communicate to other people. It seems it is not possible even to say what is impossible about them. People have, of course, tried to put words— or pictures or music—to their experience. I will have occasion later to cite many bold attempts to capture and communicate what consciousness is like.

The painter Wassily Kandinsky, whose preferred medium for celebrating consciousness was the painted canvas, had this to say about sensation: "Color is a power which directly influences the soul. Color is the keyboard, the eyes are the hammers, the soul is the piano with many strings."[10] You may or may not relate to this as true of what it is like for you. Still, Kandinsky's words at least hint at the majesty and mystery of the phenomenon.

Suppose, then, we let the epithet "soul-hammering" do duty for the description that otherwise seems so elusive. Then, *soul-hammering* is what you experience the sensation *as being*. Yet soul-hammering does not correspond to any conceivable quality of the material world. So now, again, you have two choices about the interpretation: "What I am experiencing is either (a) evidence of there being an alternative transcendental soul-hammering reality or (b) some kind of illusion."

But here is the second crucial difference. For, now, with sensations, it seems that many a person in his right mind is prepared to posit the existence of a nonphysical world just because he is confronted by an entity he cannot explain. "Everything considered, this suggests I have one foot in heaven." I am exaggerating. But not much. When in later chapters we get to explore the psychological effects of consciousness, we will see just how far the change in self-image can go.

I am running ahead. The point I want to make at this stage is that there does seem to be a formal similarity between, on the one hand, representing sensations as like something and, on the other, representing the Gregundrum as like something. Although what you make of these representations, in the larger scheme of things, is certainly different, the logic of experience is the same.

▨ Then where should we take this next? There is a philosophical term of art, "intentionality," that I think may come in useful here. Philosophers say that whenever you form a mental representation of something—when, for example, you represent object X in the world *as* object Y in your mind—the representing is an "intentional state." What the term "intentional" is meant to capture is that the representing is *about* something, it *points to* or *fingers* Y ("intendere" is Latin for "to take aim at"). Expanding on this, we can say that object Y, the thing the representing is about, is the "intentional object," whereas object X, the thing that gives rise to the representation, is the "real-world source."

In practice, the Xs and Ys sometimes come to the same thing. Using your eyes, for example, you may perceive a physical object to be pretty much what a physicist using his instruments would say it is—a cricket ball as a red leather ball, say. In that case, the distinction between the real-world source and the intentional reading collapses. But it is often the case that X and Y do not come to the same thing at all: you perceive a physical object to be something more or other than what the physicist would say it is—a piece of paper as a dollar bill, a pattern in the clouds as the face of a cat, a pile of old clothes in the bedroom as the ghost of your dead grandfather.

Then how about the Gregundrum? This is, of course, a particularly interesting and revealing case. On one hand, when you look at the Gregundrum from the special position, the object as you perceive it—which is the impossible triangle—becomes the intentional object of your perception. Meanwhile, the thing you are actually looking at, the wooden object that was constructed to deceive you, is the real-world source. On the other hand, when you look at the Gregundrum from anywhere other than the special position, then the object as you perceive it—the weird object as it physically is—becomes the intentional object of perception. And now this is in fact also the real-world source. Thus, if we return to the situation illustrated in figure 3, we find that for Observer A the intentional object and the real-world source are nothing like each other, whereas for Observer B they coincide.

Chapter 2

What, now, if consciousness were to be an illusion of a similar kind? Would this not mean we ought, in the case of consciousness too, to make a distinction between the intentional object and the real-world source? Exactly. Then let us do it.

Let us suppose that when you have a sensation, when it is like something for you to see red, for example, this mysterious thing it is like is "the intentional object of consciousness." Then there has to be a real-world source for this—some physical activity in your brain that you, from your special position as the conscious subject, engage with and represent as having the phenomenal properties. But assuming, as before, that this is not an accident, this brain activity would have to be nothing less than some kind of "sensational Gregundrum," something that has been created precisely so as to give rise to the consciousness illusion.

What and where could this wonderful thing be? Actually we already got halfway to identifying it a few paragraphs back. "You look at a ripe tomato, for example, and in response to the red light reaching your eyes, something happens in your brain that you experience as the sensation of red." But the phrase "something happens" is much too weak, and "in response to the red light" is too weak too. Sensation does, of course, have specifically *sensory* qualities, so we can safely assume the brain activity in question is typically some kind of a response to stimulation of the sense organs. But sensation—as we will see in the next chapter—is nothing if it is not *personal* and *affect laden*. So I would say the brain activity that constitutes the sensational Gregundrum must be something that *you create* in response to what the stimulation arriving at your body surface *means for you*. But this rather changes the picture. It suggests that the thing to which you are attributing those marvelous esoteric properties is in fact your own creation, something *you are doing*. Thus, if you are being tricked by an illusionist, it is not by an outside agent, no Richard Gregory scheming in his lab; it is by some part of yourself. The sensational Gregundrum is really an *ipsundrum* (from the Latin *ipse,* "self").

"Ipsundrum" is what I will, from now on, call this hypothesized, illusion-generating inner creation in response to sensory stimulation. It is an odd sort of word. But I am not unhappy with that. It is an odd sort of thing.

■ So there we are. We wanted a theory of how "it is like something" to be conscious of sensations. And now we have one. Consciousness is a magical mystery show that you lay on for yourself. You respond to sensory input by creating, as a personal response, a seemingly otherworldly object, an ipsundrum, which you present to yourself in your inner theater. Watching from the royal box, as it were, you find yourself transported to that other world.

I know that philosophers in recent years have mocked the idea of there being a so-called Cartesian Theater, where the brain creates a picture of the outside world for the edification of the mind. Daniel Dennett, the leading critic, writes: "The persuasive imagery of the Cartesian Theater keeps coming back to haunt us—laypeople and scientists alike—even after its ghostly dualism has been denounced and exorcized."[11] He is right, of course, to reject the idea that there could be a place inside your head where one part of your brain creates a faithful replica of the world for another part of your brain to look at (and what part of your brain would look at the replica of the replica?). But let us note that, despite its entry into the philosophical literature, this is a bad use of the word "theater," and it is certainly not the kind of theater I am now proposing.

Replication is not what theaters are about. Instead, theaters are places where events are staged in order to *comment* in one way or another on the world—to educate, persuade, entertain. In this sense, the idea that one part of your brain might stage a theatrical show in order to influence the judgment of another part of your brain is perfectly reasonable—indeed, biologically reasonable, as we will see.[12]

3 Sentition

Consciousness is a self-created entertainment for the mind? A show that dramatically changes your outlook on life, so as to help you—however indirectly—to propagate your genes?

I may say I have some hopes for this theory, once we have properly fleshed it out. However, I do not expect everyone to be convinced it is a good idea just yet. And among the several reasons why you would be right to be skeptical would be this. As things stand, this is a theory that would seem to have been invented for the sole purpose of "saving the phenomena"; in other words, providing a plausible explanation of the facts in front of us—namely, the curious things people say and imply about the inner state they are in when they are having sensations. What is lacking are any ancillary reasons to believe it is a *true* account.[1]

I would argue that even if this is all our theory can do—save the phenomena—this would be a major advance, since there is no competing theory that can do so much. I would go further and suggest that if we were to build a humanoid robot on these lines, with its own designed inner theater where self-generated illusory sensory objects—ipsundrums—were on show, this robot might be able to pass itself off as being phenomenally conscious; it would make all the right claims about the soul-hammering qualities of its experience, ineffability, privileged access, and so on.[2] But why say "pass itself off"? Arguably, this would amount to the real thing. The building of such a robot would certainly be an advance too.

Yet I realize we want more than this; we want our theory to be true not of robots but of human beings and other conscious creatures as they have evolved here on Earth. Which means we must show, if we can, how it relates to what we already know of the evolution of animal nervous systems. This theory of consciousness as a stage show will deserve to be taken much more seriously if we can argue that before consciousness ever arose, animals were already engaging in some kind of inner monitoring of their own responses to sensory stimulation. If this is indeed how things started, then it will be relatively easy to argue that sensations acquired their new and amazing properties by the accepted Darwinian route of "descent with modification."

It has to be said that no one knows for sure how things started. We do not have an authoritative, empirically grounded account of what the early evolutionary history of sensation was. But there have been recent attempts by scientists and philosophers—including me—to reconstruct this history from first principles.[3] So, I am now going to give you a summary sketch of my own version (with the assurance that the missing parts of the story can be found elsewhere).[4]

■ Let me start with some definitions and distinctions.

What *is* sensation? In modern human beings, sensation—for all its special phenomenal features—is still essentially the way in which you represent *your interaction with the environmental stimuli that touch your body*: red light at your eyes, sugar on your tongue, pressure on your skin, and so on. It is important to recognize that sensation is not the same thing as *perception*. Perception is the way you represent *the objective world out there beyond your body*: the chair in the kitchen, the tall tree in the garden, the thunder booming in the night sky. Sensation, by contrast, is always about what is happening *to you* and how *you feel* about it: "the pain is in my toe *and horrible*," "the sweet taste is on my tongue *and sickly*," "the red light is before my eyes *and stirs me up*." It is as if, in having sensations, you are both registering the fact of stimulation and expressing *your personal bodily opinion about it*—and indeed, as will emerge shortly from my analysis, I believe you are doing just that.

Now, sensation as human beings experience it is, of course, a *state of mind*: a cognitive state in which you represent things to yourself as being this way. Yet, we can assume that, historically, sensation had simpler beginnings. Indeed, we can be sure that our own far-distant ancestors must have been *sensitive* to stimuli, reacting to environmental stimulation in a purely reflex way, long before they had anything that could be called a mind.

We can be sure of it not least because we can still see evidence of mindless sensitivity all around us. In fact, one of the great branches of life on Earth never took things further. Many plants today show adaptive bodily responses to stimuli—opening their petals to the sun, drooping at the touch of a predator, closing their jaws to trap an insect, leaning over in the direction of a suitable host. A plant's responses can show discrimination and purposiveness. We might even say they are a behavioral expression of how the plant evaluates the stimulus: the daisy *welcomes* the sun, the mimosa *recoils* from the deer's attention. Except, of course, that these evaluations are hard-wired and automatic. No feelings are involved.[5]

We should assume, then, that our distant ancestors—let's suppose them to be, say, wormlike creatures living in the Cambrian seas—were in this respect like plants. They too would have reacted expressively to stimulation, in ways that took precise account of the nature of the stimulus and how they evaluated it. But, at least to begin with, it would have been a mindless activity: expression without mental representation.

Unlike plants, however, our ancestors were mobile and free-living animals. They found themselves living in a relatively fast-changing and complex world. Thus, even while they continued to show set patterns of response, they must, soon enough, have come under pressure to raise their game by developing more "thoughtful" kinds of behavior. They needed not just to respond reflexly, but to form some kind of internal picture of what they were responding to, so that they could begin to engage in cognitive planning and decision making. Yet, how to go about creating this mental picture, given where they had gotten to already?

The answer was beautifully simple. When an organism is already doing something about a stimulus reaching its body surface, something specifically tailored to the particular stimulus and its significance, then what the organism is doing is potentially highly informative about what the stimulus *is* and also *what it means*. Indeed, the expressive response as such is, to anyone who cares to read it, already *a form of representation*. It comes preloaded, as it were, with *aboutness* and *intentionality*.

Think of how much you could tell about what is affecting a man's body by observing his behavior when, for example, he flicks an insect from his arm, winces and covers his ears on hearing the shriek of chalk on the blackboard, or savors a chocolate in his mouth. For that matter, think what you could learn by observing how the petals of a flower open and close as the light changes.[6]

But if *you* could tell so much from the outside, then in principle *so too could the subject who is making the response*. Indeed, if the subject were to have no other way of knowing what was happening to his own body and how he felt about it, he could find out by observing his own behavior. What is more, since it is *his* behavior, he would not have to observe it from the outside; he could do it by monitoring the motor command signals he is issuing from his brain (perhaps by means of an "efference copy"—a copy of the signals that has been shunted to the side just for this purpose). The subject would, in effect, have elevated his own behavior to the level of a *performance* that he himself can read—not yet something that he is specifically staging for that purpose, but nonetheless a de facto source of information about what is going on.

The subject could find out like this in principle. And we have good reasons to believe that this is precisely how the first animals to form representations of what was happening to them did find out in practice. Chief among these reasons is the fact that sensations, as human beings experience them today, still show all the signs of having been originally a representation of *self-generated bodily activity*. We may note, especially, how both sensations and bodily actions (i) *belong* to the subject, (ii) implicate *part of his body*, (iii) are *present tense*, (iv) have a *qualitative modality*, and (v) have properties that are *phenomenally immediate*. (For readers who want to go further, these resemblances are spelled out in more detail in the notes.)[7]

Yet, if monitoring the command signals for expressive responses was indeed the start of the story, the evolution of sensation clearly did not rest there. In the early days, the responses were real bodily responses, wriggles of acceptance or rejection. The animal reacted to *this* stimulus with the equivalent of a scowl, to *that* with a welcoming smile. But humans today show little, if any, overt bodily response to most sensory stimuli. In fact, it is clear that far in the past, long before humans came on the scene, these overt responses disappeared from view. And yet humans still feel the stimulation. What happened?

What happened, I suggest, was that natural selection did some tidying up. There must have come a point in the course of evolution when the original expressive responses made by our ancestors were no longer appropriate. At this point, other things being equal, these responses would soon have been completely eliminated. However, by this point *other things were not equal* because the animal had become reliant on using the information contained in the responses as the basis for its mental representation of the stimulation at its body surface.

Now, if the animal had been monitoring its responses by observing from the outside, there would have been no way of both eliminating the responses and preserving access to this information. However, if the animal were in fact monitoring not the actual behavior but the motor command signals, there was a neat solution. This was that the responses should be *internalized*—or, as I have put it, *privatized*.

How to do this? Given the requirement that the responses should continue to carry relevant information about the stimulus, they still had to implicate the locus of stimulation on the body somehow. But this could be achieved without too radical a transformation by converting the responses into *virtual responses* at loci on a *virtual body*. Therefore, what occurred, I suggest, was that the responses began to get short-circuited before they reached the body surface, becoming targeted instead at points closer and closer in on the incoming sensory nerves, until eventually the whole process became closed off as an internal circuit within the brain. In fact, as things now stand in creatures like ourselves, the outgoing command signals now project only as far as the body maps at the level of the sensory cortex, where they interact with the incoming signals from the sense organs to create, momentarily, a self-entangling loop (see figure 4).

The upshot is that when today you experience sensory stimulation, you are still responding to it—behind the scenes—with something like the ancient pattern of bodily expression handed down from distant ancestors. The response still retains vestiges of its original evaluative function, its intentionality

| Local response occurs at site of stimulation | Response becomes targeted on incoming sensory pathway | Response becomes "privatized" within the brain |

Figure 4.

and hedonic tone. But now it has become a *virtual expression* occurring at the level of a *virtual body*, hidden inside your head. Now it is indeed *a kind of pantomime*—something whose purpose is no longer to *do* anything about the stimulation but only to *tell* about it. Action has become *acting*.

I have given a name to these internalized responses: "sentition." This name—somewhere between sensation, expression, and exhibition—is meant to capture the creative and staged quality of the response. More particularly, I have spoken of the response to red light at your eyes, for example, as "redding," to salt on your tongue as "salting," to noxious stimulation on your skin as "paining," and so on.

And where is the sensation you experience at the end of all this? Sensation is where it has been since early on: sensation is sentition—the privatized expressive activity—*as monitored by your mind*. Figure 5 illustrates how it works. Red light reflected from a tomato arrives at your eyes, and you create an internalized expressive response; you engage in redding. You monitor what you are doing so as to discover what is happening to you. And the representation you form of your own re-

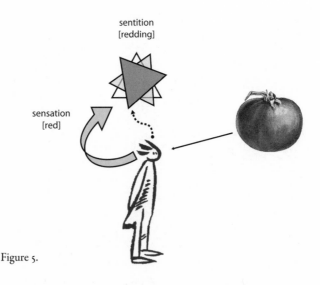

sentition
[redding]

sensation
[red]

Figure 5.

sponse is the sensation of red. Thus, for you to have the sensation of red means nothing other than for you *to observe your own redding.*

■ This, then, I suggest was the history of sensation, up to— but not yet at—the crucial point where the subject began to represent his sensory responses as having mysterious *phenomenal qualities.* Can we now see how this astonishing new development would have come about?

I will not say it is all there yet. But it is surely looking good. We wanted reassurance that the idea of consciousness as a *self-generated show* could be supported by what we might separately conclude about how sensation has evolved. Now the evolutionary story is telling us that the ancestors of human beings and other conscious creatures, since far back, have indeed been showcasing their sensory responses—just so as to learn from this how their bodies are being stimulated.

There is no reason to think that this internal monitoring of sensory responses will *in itself* have been sufficient to bring on consciousness. For the fact is that sentition, to begin with, will simply have been a handed-down form of bodily expression that will not have had any of the fancy properties that we hypothesize are responsible for generating the subjective illusion of being in the presence of mysterious qualia. Sentition, in other words, will not—yet—have become that strange thing the *ipsundrum*.

This implies, of course, that our ancestors were nonconscious before they were conscious; what is more, that they were nonconscious even after they began to form mental representations of sensory stimulation and so could be deemed to be fully sentient. This may strike us as a strange idea. What would it be like to have *nonphenomenal sensations*—sensations that provide you with all the requisite information, but without any of the phenomenal quality you take for granted? What would it be like, if I may put it so, to have SENSATIONS as opposed to SENSATIONS? The answer has to be that it would be "like" nothing in Nagel's sense of the term. This may be hard, if not impossible, for us to imagine. Still, it is certainly a consequence of the theory that this was the situation early on. Moreover, presumably this continues to be the situation of many sentient animals today. Animals that have not come under specific selection pressure to move to the next stage and generate the consciousness illusion—worms, fish, frogs—will not have done so.

But some did! I wrote just now that sentition will not—*as yet*—have become that strange thing the ipsundrum. But the "as yet" is why it is looking so good for our theory. For surely we can claim that by the time preconscious creatures

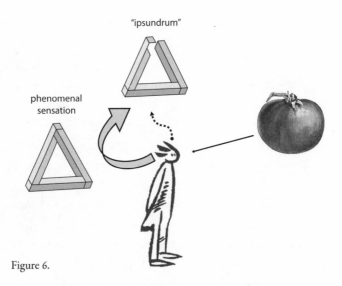

"ipsundrum"

phenomenal
sensation

Figure 6.

had evolved to the point shown in figure 5, the ground was laid. At this point sentition will have been perfectly placed to take on an enhanced new role, being already a stage show of sorts, possibly needing only new direction to become a *magical* stage show.

Figure 6—where I have taken literally the analogy between the ipsundrum and the Gregundrum—illustrates what our theory predicts happened next. You will see that the activity of redding has taken on a remarkable new look.

4 Looping the Loop

So, the idea now is that, in the course of evolution, the illusion-generating ipsundrum was conjured up *out of* sentition. And our two questions must be: What happened, in terms of brain engineering, to bring about this remarkable advance? And why did natural selection favor this development? In this chapter I will offer a suggestion about *what*. The rest of the book will be devoted to the question *why*.

I cannot pretend to know what exactly went on at the level of the brain. This will therefore be the least confident—and possibly the most throwaway—chapter in the book. But you would expect me to have *something* to say about the structural basis of the innovation that I am arguing changed everything. And so I will.

I feel justified in sharing some highly speculative ideas with you on two grounds. First, I am convinced that, since the ipsundrum has to be a real-world object, in the sense I defined earlier, it must be within the capacity of science to describe it. The neuroscientists Francis Crick and Christof Koch have written: "The most difficult aspect of consciousness is the so-called 'hard problem' of qualia—the redness of red, the painfulness of pain, and so on. No one has produced any plausible explanation as to how the experience of the redness of red could arise from the actions of the brain. It appears fruitless to approach this problem head-on."[1] But I rather believe the opposite is true: if we do not venture, we will not gain.

Second, I think it will be not too serious a matter if we get the answer wrong. At least getting it wrong need not compromise our discussion of the functional benefits of consciousness, which will come later in the book. Let the ipsundrum really be made of chalk while we conclude it is made of cheese, and we can still go on to ask all the right questions about what biological advantage creating the ipsundrum brings (which, incidentally, allows me the luxury of saying—and meaning it—that if you find parts of the argument of the next few pages hard going, then it is okay to skip them and go straight to chapter 5).

My starting point is that whatever was done to sentition, it cannot have been *much*. Natural selection works by modifying existing structures, and then only in easily available steps. Given that sentition was already an internalized kind of bodily expression, then this must have been the clay from which the ipsundrum was modeled.

What I would like to do theoretically is to "reverse engineer" this process. Ideally, this would mean we should begin with what we want to explain as the end product, namely sensation with its phenomenal qualities as human beings experience it today. Then we should work out what kind of real-world object could possibly support this illusory experience. And then we should try to trace the evolution of this structure backward. Hopefully, at the end we should have discovered a route by which, through a series of relatively minor quantitative changes in sentition, a major qualitative change could have been brought about in how it gets to be represented. I cannot say this has been my strategy exactly. But you will recognize the spirit of it in what follows.

Let us turn then to the phenomenology of sensation, with a degree of attention we have not given it so far.

Consider any moment of sensory consciousness you will. Drinking a cup of breakfast coffee. Rain falling on your head. The sting of a stinging nettle. Staring at a starlit sky. *This*—whatever "this" is that you are pointing to in your experience—is how you, a human being, are representing the ipsundrum you are creating. *This,* we are assuming, will not be what the real-world object actually is, but it is *what it is like.*

Now, sensation, we can all agree, has special qualities on a variety of levels. Let me list the most salient (while offering excuses, as always, for the inadequacy of the language here).

- There is the sense you have of *being there*, present and embodied, and yet as if on a separate plane of existence from the physical world that carries you.
- There is the feeling of *singularity*, of occupying a place in the universe that cannot be accessed by anyone or anything else.

- There is the paradoxical sense of living outside the physical instant, as if in a moment of *thick subjective time*.
- There is the *quality space* you have entered, where every sensation is created out of a sense-organ-specific medium—light, sound, taste, smell, touch—with a seemingly unbridgeable gulf between these sensory domains.
- There is the strangely unjustifiable—unjustifiable because to human reason *unquestionable*—nature of all this.
- There is the wondrous beauty of it all.

The ipsundrum must have a lot to answer for if it gives rise to such a many-layered entertainment. We can safely say there can be few types of real-world objects that could generate an illusion on this scale: not just a one-trick pony, but a complete *cirque fantastique*. Yet, conscious beings are living testament that there was *one* type of object that could do it. And if natural selection found it, and found it merely by modifying sentition, then so I hope can we.

I will not tease you by holding back my answer. I think the secret is that the ipsundrum is not so much a physical object as a mathematical object. It is a complex dynamic pattern of activity in neural circuits whose special properties are realized and become "visible" only at the level of a *computation that integrates what happens over time.* In short, the ipsundrum is a bit like a developing thunderstorm, a bit like a wheeling flock of starlings, a bit like a musical sonata.

I suggest that what is supporting this pattern of activity at the brain level is the existence of *reentrant feedback loops*—

loops that allow the activity initiated by external stimulation to become, for a brief while at least, self-sustaining. Such feedback would have been a relatively easy thing for natural selection to arrange, because the ground had already been laid by the privatization of sentition. Since the earliest days, when the sensory responses were an overt kind of bodily expression, these responses would have been influencing the stimulation to which they were a response, so the potential for feedback was already there (think, for example, of what happens when you scratch an itch). To begin with, the feedback would have been too uncoordinated and slow to have had any interesting emergent properties. However, once sentition became internalized and the return pathway much shortened (see figure 4 in the last chapter), conditions would have been ripe for the activity in the circuit to catch its own tail and so begin to cycle around and around.

Then, all at once, things will have been ready to take off. Once there is *recursion* in a loop like this, the potential will be there for generating dynamic patterns with properties that are very strange indeed. All that has to happen is that each time the activity cycles around the circuit, the transmission characteristics of the circuit are altered *by this activity.* In that case, the way in which the activity develops in each new cycle will depend on the level of activity the previous time around. The growth of activity in such a circuit will be governed by what is called "a delay differential equation." A delay differential equation (DDE) is an equation where the evolution of the system at a certain time, t, say, depends on the state of the system at an earlier time, t-T, say.

What happens then is that the activity, once started, if it does not quickly die away, will either develop chaotically,

Looping the Loop

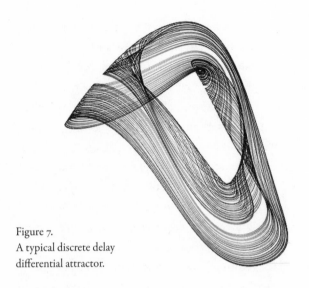

Figure 7.
A typical discrete delay
differential attractor.

never settling down, or soon settle into a "basin of attraction"—an "attractor state" in which the same pattern repeats
itself indefinitely and to which it returns even if disturbed.
Figure 7 shows a simple example of an attractor state, where
the stable pattern can be described by the path of a line in a
three-dimensional graph.[2] However, typically the attractor
will turn out to be very much more complicated and will occupy a higher-dimensional landscape. That is, while the pattern is still stable and has a precise mathematical description,
it would require a graph with more than three dimensions to
portray it. The number of additional dimensions can be very
large indeed. In fact, there will be cases where it would require
a graph with an infinite number of dimensions.

But is this not exactly the kind of thing we have been
looking for?[3] Suppose that natural selection, in designing the
ipsundrum, had all those extra dimensions to play with. The
mind boggles (perhaps literally) at the possibilities for creat-

ing mathematical objects in the brain that when "seen" by an internal observer, would give rise to the illusion of something with extraordinary otherworldly properties.

Of course, insofar as the ipsundrum must be observed from a unique position for the illusion to work, natural selection would also have had to arrange for the internal observer to have this special perspective. But, now it comes to it, I wonder whether perhaps this condition could be relaxed. It is an intrinsic feature of attractors that they are resistant to perturbation: they are indeed "basins" into which things tend to fall, so that the developing activity ends up in the same state, no matter where it started from. Arguably, this very feature could have been exploited so as to give the ipsundrum the same illusionary look no matter where it was seen from. I wrote earlier, in relation to the Gregundrum, let us suppose "that things are rigged so that, as and when you move around the object, some hidden hand turns it so that it is always facing you in the same way." Would it not be neat if this could be taken care of automatically, so that from the point of view of the internal observer the ipsundrum as a mathematical object is "self-positioning"?

At any rate, without more ado let me propose that this is the solution. What natural selection did to bring consciousness onstage was nothing other than to adjust the properties of existing sensory feedback loops so as to steer the activity toward a special class of attractor states—just such states as would seem, from the subject's point of view, to give sensations their phenomenal qualities.

◼ These are nice ideas. But I would have to agree they are still very loosely formulated. And I am sure you would want me to make some more specific suggestions before you come onboard. So let me discuss one prominent feature of sensation that I believe can be explained—perhaps can *only* be explained—along these lines. It is a feature we have already identified as a key element of sensory phenomenology, and one that many commentators have considered fundamental. This is the peculiar way that *time* enters in.

Imagine yourself looking at a cascading waterfall or listening to the song of a skylark. Physical time is flowing linearly forward, with no letup in the relentless passage from instant to instant. The stimuli that are reaching your sense organs are always changing. Many a new stimulus is over just as soon as it arrives.

But this is not how you experience it at the level of sensation. Rather, the present moment, the "now" of sensation, has a paradoxical dimension of temporal depth. Each instance of sensation is still there for you for a brief period after you create it, as if it happens *for longer than it happens.* Thus successive instances are co-present in consciousness. But this is not because the old is lasting into the time territory of the new; it is because each new instance lives on for a little while in its own time. You have co-presence of sensations without simultaneity.

The paradoxical status of time in the experience of sensations has been remarked on since the dawn of philosophy. Aristotle, in his book *Of the Senses,* struggled—as we still do—to describe it. Here is a modern commentary on what Aristotle meant to say: "The undivided 'now' of sensation must rest upon a duration with which it does not altogether coincide; the present moment must conceal, within itself, the passing of another, immeasurable by its own standard. . . . It is another time; to the degree to which time cannot admit of varieties of itself, it may well be something other than any time at all."[4]

We may well ask: What is going on? What could possibly give rise to the illusion—for of course it must be an illusion—that the past is still present, as if you are living in "thick time"? Can we imagine some kind of ipsundrum that would appear to the subject to endure without ever getting older? Is there a type of attractor that could take us there?

Because of Douglas Hofstadter's groundbreaking work in a related area, I believe there is an answer we can take right off the peg. Hofstadter has pioneered the analysis of a special class of feedback relationship that he calls a "strange loop."[5] This exists in a system when there are several layers of operation, the higher layers being built upon the lower, but in which the higher layers are capable of reaching down and changing the structure or rules of the lower levels. Cyclic activity in such a loop is again described by a delay differential equation, but in this case with a particularly remarkable outcome. In Hofstadter's words, the outcome, for someone observing it, is that "in the series of stages that constitute the cycling-around, there is a shift from one level of abstraction (or structure) to another, which feels like an upwards movement in a hierarchy, and yet somehow the successive 'upward' shifts turn out to give rise to a closed cycle. That is, despite one's sense of departing ever further from one's origin, one winds up, to one's shock, exactly where one had started out."[6]

What would this be like for the observer on the inside? Well, if you want a visual spatial metaphor, it might be like climbing an endless staircase that always takes you back to the same place you set off from (figure 8). Or if it is to be an auditory metaphor, it might be like listening to a glissando where the sound seems always to be falling or rising in pitch without the note ever changing (you can hear such an amazing glissando online).[7]

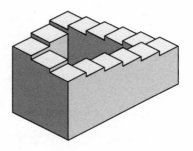

Figure 8.

But where might "unused time" come in? Let us look at it this way. If you climb the staircase in figure 8 and end up exactly at the *height* you started out, we would conventionally describe this as having traveled *no distance* upward. But space and time are equivalent in this peculiar situation. So, if you climb the staircase and end up exactly where you set out *earlier*, an equally good interpretation would be that you have passed *no time*. Indeed imagine you were to measure time by counting how many steps you have ascended: one second, two second, three seconds . . . *no* seconds. You would have *spent* time, without *using* it.

Now, to translate this back to sensation. Suppose that, in responding to a sensory stimulus, you were to initiate activity in a feedback loop whose attractor turned out to be just such a strange mathematical object. Then, when you monitored yourself doing this—and found yourself creating something that from your first-person viewpoint would appear to be the temporal analogue of an endless staircase—is it not possible that you would find yourself having the experience of living in the thick moment?

I do not know. But I daresay you might. In figure 9 I have tried to illustrate how it could work. You will see (if you can follow the diagrammatic convention) that things have moved on again since figure 6. The activity of redding has now acquired the interesting new property of seeming to the subject to exist in its own virtual time.

This is not, of course, all we need to explain the subjective properties of qualia. But it is surely not a bad start. And having made this start, I think we can see how we might take it further by adding appropriate bells and whistles to sentition. If, as theorists, we can describe just what it is that, as a feature of sensory phenomenology, we want to add, I would hazard that it ought to be within the power of the mathematics of complex dynamical systems to deliver it as the property of an attractor state. And in that case we are home and dry. For we can safely assume it would have been within the power of natural selection to create this attractor by playing around with the design of the sensory feedback loops. Of course, *describing what we want to add* will still be half the battle (though I think we will make some progress with this as the book proceeds).

Figure 9.

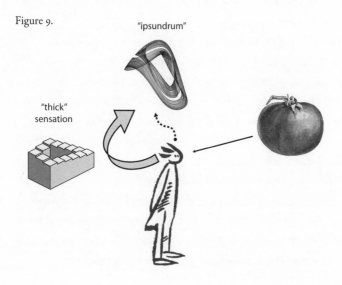

"ipsundrum"

"thick" sensation

At any rate, who says, now, that it cannot be done, that "we cannot so much as imagine the solution of the hard problem"? I should not say this, but I will say it anyway: it is a good thing that natural selection did not give up on the search for the ipsundrum so easily. Just *how good a thing*, I hope to show in the pages that follow.

■ Meanwhile, where is the Andromedan scientist in all this? I have not forgotten her. Let's suppose—if you will suspend your reasonable skepticism—that these ideas about the physical basis of consciousness are basically correct. Should we expect the Andromedan to discover the existence of this kind of ipsundrum when she examines the human brain? And will she realize its significance?

I will start with the second part of this. Will she realize its significance? As we discussed at the end of the first chapter, unless consciousness is some kind of uncaused miracle, once an outside scientist has identified the brain events that correspond to the subjective experience of sensations—the neural correlate of consciousness, the NCC—then, provided she is in possession of the neurophenomenological rule book, she ought, in principle, to be able to see that these events must lead to the subject's having just the experiences he has. Now we are suggesting that the NCC is in fact the set of brain events that occur when the subject observes, from a certain privileged position, his own ipsundrum, which is the integral of the activity in a special kind of feedback loop. So, yes, why not? If and when the Andromedan has identified this particular set of brain events as the NCC, she ought to be able to deduce what it must be like to be the subject, and so she will indeed realize exactly how significant the ipsundrum is.

But, we have to ask, *will* she be able identify this set of brain events as the NCC to begin with? Let us assume she has taken an interest in the evolutionary story. She has understood how sentition has been internalized, and she has picked up on the existence of sensory feedback circuits. She may even have noticed how the activity in these circuits tends to settle into higher-dimensional attractor states (although this may not be easy for her, it is not exactly going to show up as colored patches on an MRI scan).

However, here is the difficulty: unless and until *she happens to put herself at the subject's position* and so see for herself the magical illusion that is being created from his point of view, she is unlikely to think anything very remarkable is occurring. Even if, as I suggested a few paragraphs back, the ipsundrum as a mathematical object has been designed to be "self-positioning" from the point of view of the first-person subject, this is unlikely to be at all obvious from the outside.

So, the problem for the Andromedan is that she is going to require either extraordinary prescience or extraordinary luck, because without it she is simply not going to appreciate what the ipsundrum is *designed to do*. There is surely a lesson for experimental scientists here on Earth, for if the Andromedan would have such problems with recognizing the ipsundrum as something significant, worth further investigation, then so will they. It goes to show, I would say, that we cannot wait for advances in neuroscience to solve the problem of consciousness. Crick and Koch, in the passage I quoted earlier, continued: "It appears fruitless to approach this problem head-on. Instead we are attempting to find the neural correlate(s) of consciousness (NCC), in the hope that when we can explain the NCC in causal terms, this will make the problem of qualia clearer." Good luck to them. But I suspect that finding the NCC experimentally will be even more difficult than approaching the problem head on. The probability is that brain scientists would not recognize the NCC for what it is even if it were right in front of them.

I know there are scholars who will—and do—tut-tut at my own way of proceeding in this chapter: by trying to *think* things through. The geneticist, Steve Jones, once wrote in relation to some earlier ideas of mine: "I have a problem with scientists who spend time looking at their own navels. . . . My feeling about [most scientists who have gone into the field of consciousness studies] is that they'd find life more interesting if they continued to do what most of them started by doing—getting their feet wet by doing experimental work."[8] He memorably added: "I often think that philosophy is to science as pornography is to sex, I mean it's cheaper and easier and some people seem to prefer it."

This is all very well. Yes, of course we should use experimental evidence when we can. But if—as with consciousness—we have as yet almost no inkling as to what we should be looking for, and if, as I am now suggesting, we would probably miss it even if we did, then we ought not to be embarrassed to make use of pure theory. This is one problem that really may be best approached from an armchair.

However, the same is not true of where I will go next in this book. This is: to the big question of why consciousness—whatever its brain basis—has been selected during the course of evolution. Of course, this is a question that can be answered only by attending to the facts: the facts about what difference consciousness makes to the survival of those who have it.

PART TWO

5 So What?

I have tried, in part 1 of this book, to do what no one has done before: to explain how phenomenal consciousness could be an evolved feature of the human mind. My particular suggestions about the brain basis may be wrong. But in putting them on the table, I hope I have persuaded you that a naturalistic explanation of consciousness is at least a possibility in principle.

My theory is not quite the "transparent theory" that has been called for, "one that, once you get it, you see that anything built like *this* will have *this* particular conscious experience." But it is getting there. I would say we have every reason to believe that if a human being *were to have evolved to be built like this,* he would end up thinking, saying, and doing all of the right things for us to suppose him conscious—and of course for him to suppose it too. What is more, a human being *could have evolved to be built like this,* because there would have been a natural trajectory through the biological design space, leading him from primitive ancestors to where he is today.

So now let us put the question of *what* behind us. Now the challenge is to explain the purpose of it all. We can be sure it did not happen accidentally. It must be the result of natural selection favoring genes that underwrite the specialized neural circuits—whatever they actually are—that sustain the illusion of qualia, giving rise to the magical mystery show for the first person. And it is axiomatic that this will have happened only if those lucky enough to be spectators of this show have somehow been at an advantage in terms of biological survival compared with their less fortunate cousins.

In chapter 1 I mentioned the idea of a philosophical zombie—the philosophers' fantasy of a creature who is physically identical to a normal human being but completely lacks conscious experience. "Philosophical zombies look and behave like the conscious beings that we know and love, but 'all is dark inside.'"[1] I gave reasons for saying that, in principle, philosophical zombies do not and could not exist. However, it has to be part of my evolutionary argument that these zombies have a near relation that could certainly exist. We might call it a "psychological zombie." A psychological zombie, let's assume, is physically identical to a normal human being *except in one crucial respect*: namely, that he or she lacks just those evolved circuits in the brain that yield the phenomenal quality of conscious experience.

Would psychological zombies look and behave like the conscious beings that we know and love, despite the fact that all is dark inside? No, that is exactly the point. If consciousness is an evolutionary adaptation, the answer has to be that they would not. There must be things that a psychological zombie would *do* differently *precisely because all is dark inside.* And for natural selection to have seen this, this difference must result in the zombie's being less likely to survive and reproduce. Compared with a conscious human being, a psychological zombie would fail to thrive.

In the pages that follow, I will discuss, in point after point, the possible advantages that conscious creatures might have over psychological zombies. But "psychological zombie" is a cumbersome term, so I will sometimes talk simply of "zombies." Since I will be referring to creatures that are biologically credible (indeed, creatures whose like must once have existed on Earth and were outcompeted by the conscious creatures who came later in the course of evolution), I trust no one will confuse my zombies with the logically impossible and ultimately much less interesting philosophical version.[2]

But if conscious creatures did outcompete the zombies, why? What reasons are there to believe that the phenomenal richness of consciousness could play an essential part in *anything of practical value*? Here is a reminder of Flanagan's definition of "consciousness inessentialism": it is "the view that for any intelligent activity *I*, performed in any cognitive domain *d*, even if *we* do *I* with conscious accompaniments, *I* can in principle be done without these conscious accompaniments." As Fodor has colorfully put it: "[Consciousness] seems to be among the chronically unemployed. . . . What mental processes can be performed only because the mind is conscious, and what does consciousness contribute to their performance? Nobody has an answer to this question for any mental process whatsoever. As far as anybody knows, anything that our conscious minds can do they could do just as well if they weren't conscious. Why then did God bother to make consciousness?"[3]

▨ Fodor is undoubtedly asking the right question: "Why . . . did God [or natural selection] bother to make consciousness?" But I believe I know why he finds it all so baffling ("I understand his ignorance," as the poet Coleridge would say).[4] It is because he is looking at the problem from entirely the wrong angle. Note the bias in both Flanagan's and Fodor's formulations, toward thinking of consciousness as contributing to the *capacity* to do something. They are both assuming, as indeed almost everybody does, that the role of phenomenal consciousness—if it has one—must be to provide the subject with some kind of new mental *skill*. In other words, it must be helping him perform some task that he can perform *only* by virtue of being conscious—as, say, a bird can fly *only* because it has wings, or you can understand this sentence *only* because you know English.[5]

However, I have another idea. What if the role of phenomenal consciousness is not this at all? What if its role is not to *enable* you to do something you could not do otherwise but rather to *encourage* you to do something you would not do otherwise: to make you *take an interest* in things that otherwise would not interest you, *to mind* about things you otherwise would not mind about, or to *set yourself goals* you otherwise would not set?

I hedged my bets in the introductory chapter and suggested that consciousness has its effects on survival by changing what we may loosely call the subject's psychology—knowing that the term "psychology" could cover just about everything the mind is involved in, from cognition to self-expression. But from here on I want to put aside all the usual subject matter of cognitive science—intelligence, information processing, decision making, attention, and so on—where people have looked in vain for a role for consciousness, and to explore instead the impact of phenomenal experience on subjective purposes, attitudes, and values.

In short, I want to suggest that what having phenomenal experiences does is profoundly to change your worldview so as to change the direction of your life. It brings about a kind of Kuhnian paradigm shift in *your take on what it's all about.*

Thomas Kuhn, of course, was concerned with scientific revolutions: "Led by a new paradigm, scientists adopt new instruments and look in new places. Even more important, during revolutions scientists see new and different things when looking with familiar instruments in places they have looked before."[6] But what, now, if led by the consciousness paradigm, human ancestors had adopted new instruments and looked in new places? Even more important, what if they had seen new and different things when looking with familiar instruments in places their unconscious predecessors had looked before?

■ A "consciousness paradigm"? We will have to explore what this could mean in practice. What difference does being phenomenally conscious make to the way individuals think about and conduct themselves? What beliefs and attitudes flow from it? In the case of humans, if not other animals, what transformations does it bring about in the collective culture, and how do these in turn bring further changes?

These are—or ought to be—empirical questions: questions we can answer only by careful fieldwork in the realm of

So What?

conscious creatures. So we need to engage in a thoroughgoing study of the *natural history of consciousness*. And it must be a program of research in which we are ready to consider all sorts of possibilities—not just those we would expect to find discussed in the science or philosophy sections of the library but perhaps those that belong in the self-help, mind and spirit, or even New Age section.

What we have to do is what Daniel Dennett has called "heterophenomenology" (phenomenology from another's viewpoint). Here is Dennett discussing how Martian scientists might set about their consciousness fieldwork (Dennett flies in his investigators from a nearer place than I do): "Among the phenomena that would be readily observable by these Martians would be all our *public* representations of consciousness: cartoon 'thought balloons' . . . soliloquies in plays, voice-overs in films, use of the *omniscient author* point of view in novels, and so forth. . . . They would also have available to them the less entertaining representations of consciousness found in all the books by philosophers, psychologists, neuroscientists, phenomenologists, and other sober investigators of the phenomena."[7]

However, I would go further than Dennett. I think this list is still too cautious and biased toward traditional kinds of evidence. Neither he nor any other mainstream philosopher of consciousness seems to have recognized how consciousness may contribute to *personal growth*.

It is our good fortune, however, that other types of researchers have recognized this all along. We might call them the "alternative natural historians of consciousness": on one side are painters, poets, musicians; on the other, followers of meditative religious traditions, such as Buddhists. Do not be surprised, therefore, if I call artists and monks to the witness box or if I make much of direct quotations from individuals rhapsodizing about their personal experiences. The things people say—and especially the things that are remembered and quoted as seeming right and interesting to other conscious beings—provide some of the best evidence we can get about what consciousness does.

In what direction will this testimony lead? I will not hold back my main conclusion, although I expect I may shock you with how simple it is (after a lifetime of working on the question, I have shocked myself).

I think that what the natural history reveals is that consciousness—on several levels—makes *life more worth living*. Conscious creatures enjoy *being* phenomenally conscious. They enjoy *the world* in which they are phenomenally conscious. And they enjoy *their selves* for being phenomenally conscious. But "enjoy" is too weak a term. In the case of human beings, at any rate, it would be truer to say: they *revel in being* phenomenally conscious. They *love the world* in which they are phenomenally conscious. They *esteem their selves* for being phenomenally conscious.

Moreover, as I will show in the coming chapters, for conscious creatures there is real biological value in all this. The added *joie de vivre*, the new *enchantment* with the world they live in, and the novel sense of their own *metaphysical importance* has, in the course of evolutionary history, dramatically increased the investment individuals make in their own survival.

■ I say "in the case of human beings, at any rate." Should I say nonhuman animals too? And if so, which? The question of which other species are conscious, and which are sentient but unconscious—psychological zombies, in effect—is an issue we have not fully faced yet.

In presenting the evolutionary story, I have of course gone along with the standard assumption that human beings are not the first and only animals to have developed phenomenal consciousness. However, the grounds for this assumption are by no means as strong as we might wish. If there has been rather little systematic study of the natural history of consciousness in our own species, there has been still less for other animals. Indeed, if you look at Dennett's list of the evidential sources that an alien scientist (but it could equally be an Earth scientist) might use to research consciousness in humans, you will realize that not one of these sources would be available for nonhuman animals, not even a chimpanzee, let alone a mouse. Chimps simply do not go in for dramatic soliloquies and so on.

You may think it would be absurd to suggest that human beings alone have consciousness. I would agree. Evolutionary considerations rule out the possibility that the whole thing began with human beings. However, this does not mean that consciousness *just as we humans know it* is widely shared with animals.

I drew attention in the previous chapter to how sensations amaze us humans in a variety of ways. But there is certainly no reason to believe that these varieties came all at once in evolution. It is surely more probable that consciousness evolved in stages and that today there still exist animals with differing kinds and degrees of sensory qualia.

For a start, given what I have suggested about the brain basis of the ipsundrum, it would seem likely that phenomenal properties were established independently in the different sensory modalities. So, perhaps, for our distant ancestors it was "like something" to experience touch before it was "like something" to experience sound or light. And it could still be the case today that some animals have consciousness in only one modality.

But beyond this, it would seem likely that different kinds of phenomenal effects kicked in at different times: temporal thickening, the absolute separation of quality spaces, aesthetic valency, intrinsicality, privacy, ineffability... in an order we cannot yet specify (although ineffability could hardly have been an issue for prelinguistic creatures). Again, this would imply that some animals today are more richly conscious than others.

True, we might want to argue that the single most important transition was the first one: from being like *nothing* to being like *something*—and that all the rest is icing on the cake. Maybe in some sense that is right. You are either in flatland or in three dimensions; you either enter a magical nonphysical world or you do not. Arguably, the truly revolutionary development must have been when, perhaps quite soon after sentition became privatized, some chance change in its configuration first created the subjective illusion of being in the presence of something magically different. But if this was indeed the tipping point, it was still only the prelude. There would still have been a way to go before the full-blown magic show of consciousness was on the road, plenty of scope for "improving" sensations so as to make them ever more impressive.

Lacking the evidence to clinch it (though with plenty of suggestive evidence to be considered in the coming chapters), I may tell you my guess is that the self-made show did not become outrightly *soul-hammering*, in the grand sense Kandinsky was alluding to, until quite recent times—and maybe only thanks to advances that occurred specifically in the human line. Though I am jumping ahead, I will say it now: no nonhuman animals *make of* consciousness what human beings do. Consciousness may indeed contribute to a sense of self in nonhuman animals. But there is no evidence that any nonhuman animals, whatever the level of their consciousness, have gone on to invent the idea of a "person," an "I," let alone a "soul" with a life beyond the body (which is, of course, precisely why Dennett's list of the "evidences of consciousness" cannot be used with animals: they are all essentially "I" related).

How far this specifically human notion of selfhood has followed on from innovations in what sensations are like for humans—that is, primary facts about the quality of human consciousness—and how far on feedback from culture, once humanity as a cultural phenomenon came of age, are issues we have still to explore. I am sure most theorists would put their money on cultural influences. Yet the fact is that humans have evolved rapidly since they split from chimpanzees five million years ago. Their brains and minds have undergone radical rewiring. And, remarkably enough, new research in comparative anatomy shows that human brains have diverged not only in higher executive functions but also in the early stages of sensory processing. The primary visual cortex in humans has an extra layer of cells that does not exist in apes or monkeys. Todd Preuss and Ghislaine Coleman, who made the discovery, comment: "The existence of substantial differences in the organization of primary visual cortex between human and nonhuman primates (including the commonly studied macaque monkeys) may come as a surprise, given how widely held is the conviction that the human visual system is basically or essentially similar to our close relatives." There is no evidence yet as to what this extra layer is doing. The authors suggest a "low level" explanation in terms of differences in visual attention and perception of movement. But I wonder if they are not underestimating the significance of their discovery. Might not this extra layer be just what is needed to create a uniquely human kind of reverberatory loop? At least let's not rule out the possibility that the wonderfully inflated human self-image has arisen out of some more basic change in sensory phenomenology—one that has happened in the human line alone.[8]

Let's revisit this question of grades of consciousness when we know more about what exactly is at issue.

6   Being There

In the previous chapter I headlined three levels at which I believe the lives of our ancestors were transformed by consciousness, three levels at which, if we look on the negative side, we could say the lives of psychological zombies—lacking those extra brain circuits—would be impoverished compared with our own. Now in separate chapters, I will treat these one by one—beginning with the simple pleasure of *pure being*.

The bottom line about how consciousness changes the human outlook—as deep an existential truth as anyone could ask for—is this: *we do not want to be zombies*. We *like* "being present," we *like* having it "be like something to be me," and only in the most drastic circumstances would we have it otherwise.

Lord Byron says it: "The great object of life is sensation—to feel that we exist, even though in pain. It is this 'craving void' which drives us to gaming—to battle—to travel—to intemperate, but keenly felt pursuits of any description, whose principal attraction is the agitation inseparable from their accomplishment."[1]

Tom Nagel as a philosopher says it more soberly: "There are elements which, if added to one's experience, make life better; there are other elements which, if added to one's experience, make life worse. But what remains when these are set aside is not merely *neutral*: it is emphatically positive. . . . The additional positive weight is supplied by experience itself, rather than by any of its contents."[2]

John Galsworthy, in one of his Forsyte novels, describes fourteen-month-old Kit Forsyte taking a bath: "He seemed to lend a meaning to life. His vitality was absolute, not relative. His kicks and crows and splashings had the joy of a gnat's dance, or a jackdaw's gambols in the air. They gave thanks not for what he was about to receive, but for what he was receiving."[3]

■ The word "sensualism" approaches but hardly does justice to what these writers are getting at. Maybe we need the word "presentism."[4] At any rate, the emotion is a basic and familiar one: the yen to confirm and renew, in small ways or large, your own occupancy of the subjective moment, to go deeper, to extend it, to revel in being there—and, where you have the skill, to celebrate it in words.

Here is John Keats, in a letter to a friend, sharing his mouth with us: "Talking of Pleasure, this moment I am writing with one hand, and with the other holding to my Mouth a Nectarine—good god how fine—It went down soft pulpy, slushy, oozy—all its delicious embonpoint melted down my throat like a large beatified Strawberry."[5]

Or here, on a more heroic scale, is Albert Camus, inviting us to enter the skin of his young body as he luxuriates among the flower-covered Roman ruins of Tipasa on the Algerian coast: "We enter a blue and yellow world and are welcomed by the pungent, odorous sigh of the Algerian summer earth. . . . We are not seeking lessons or the bitter philosophy one requires of greatness. Everything seems futile here except the sun, our kisses, and the wild scents of the earth. . . . How many hours I have spent crushing absinthe leaves, caressing ruins, trying to match my breathing with the world's tumultuous sighs! Deep among wild scents and concerts of somnolent insects, I open my eyes and heart to the unbearable grandeur of this heat-soaked sky."[6]

Or here, to take it down to a more domestic level, is Rupert Brooke, stirring up thoughts of lesser ecstasies as he provides an inventory of one small sensory delicacy after another.

These I have loved:
White plates and cups, clean-gleaming,
Ringed with blue lines; and feathery, faery dust;
Wet roofs, beneath the lamp-light; the strong crust
Of friendly bread; and many-tasting food;
Rainbows; and the blue bitter smoke of wood;
And radiant raindrops couching in cool flowers;
And flowers themselves, that sway through sunny hours,
Dreaming of moths that drink them under the moon.

The list is long. The poet fondles each moment, like a bead on a rosary.

Then, the cool kindliness of sheets, that soon
Smooth away trouble; and the rough male kiss
Of blankets; grainy wood; live hair that is
Shining and free; blue-massing clouds; the keen
Unpassioned beauty of a great machine;
The benison of hot water; furs to touch;
The good smell of old clothes; and other such—
The comfortable smell of friendly fingers,
Hair's fragrance, and the musty reek that lingers
About dead leaves and last year's ferns. . . .[7]

He is only just beginning, and I will return to this astonishing paean to sensation in a later chapter. But in reading this
and the passages before it, I want to remark how rooted in
the natural world all these precious experiences are. There is
nothing in Keats's or Camus' descriptions, and only the oc-
casional item in Brooke's, that has any contemporary cultural
reference. Absinthe leaves, blue massing clouds, moist earth,
and so on, have, since time immemorial, been freely on offer
to anyone with the senses and the inner leisure to appreciate
them. We can and should assume, therefore, that our human
ancestors of 100,000 years ago, or maybe as much as a million,
relished many of these same experiences.

But then perhaps we should assume that the emotion I just
now called presentism does in fact go back much further and
spreads much wider. There is no lack of evidence that many
nonhuman animals have evolved, at some level, to like "being
there" just as humans do—which strongly suggests that they
experience a qualia-rich version of the subjective present, basically like ours.

Galsworthy, looking for an analogy for the boy in his bath, went straight to animals: "the joy of a gnat's dance, or a jackdaw's gambols in the air." And there are, of course, animal parallels to be drawn on every side, not just for Kit Forsyte but also for Keats, Camus, Brooke, and even Nagel. Dolphins surf the waves. Dogs chase their tails in frenzy. Bonobos give each other erotic body rubs. Cats stretch themselves before the fire. Lambs frolic on the spring sward. Monkeys leap from high cliffs into water pools.

At the Gombe Stream Research Centre in Tanzania, a chimpanzee beside a stream was observed by scientists drawing her fingers repeatedly through the rippling water, transfixed, it seems, by the delicate play of light, sound, and touch on her body. Other chimps began to copy her, and within months this kind of water play had become a family tradition. "Sitting intently nearby was Golden, who watched for a time before mimicking Gaia's exact motions. Playing in Kakombe Stream, the field team observes, has since become something of a Gremlin family tradition: Every time they cross the creek, Golden finds time to sit on a rock with her hand immersed in the water, overturning stones on the streambed."[8] But at Gombe scientists have also observed examples of much wilder, Byronic sensation seeking, as when a chimpanzee emerges into the open in a thunderstorm and dances and stamps and screams as torrents of rain run from his back and lightning forks the air.

Marc Bekoff describes: "I once saw a young elk in Rocky Mountain National Park run across a snowfield, jump in the air and twist his body while in flight, stop, catch his breath and do it again and again. Buffalo have been seen playfully running onto and sliding across ice, excitedly bellowing as they do so."[9] George Schaller describes a two-year-old panda on being released from a dark tunnel: "It exploded with joy. Exuberantly it trotted up an incline with a high-stepping, lively gait, bashing down any bamboo in its path, then turned and somersaulted down, an ecstatic black and white ball rolling over and over; then it raced back up to repeat the descent, and again."[10]

Birds are up there too, as this account reveals:

> A common feature of the hot, dry inland of Australia is the dust devil or willy-nilly, a small vortex with winds about 60 kilometres per hour. It can carry dust hundreds of metres into the air. . . . A common native bird, the galah, has been seen flying into these whirlwinds and being hurled upwards, screeching loudly. On reaching the top, the galahs fly down and enjoy another ride by re-entering the vortex near the ground. There is one report of a flock of galahs flying into a much less common and more dangerous tornado. The winds, spinning at over 100 kilometres per hour, immediately spat them out, screeching with delight.[11]

"To feel that you exist—even though in pain"? It certainly looks that way.

▪ So here is the question. Why should feeling that you exist—and valuing the feeling—be biologically adaptive, so that the underlying brain circuits would have been selected in the course of evolution?

I believe the answer (at least the beginning of an answer) is right there in front of us. It is that a creature who takes pleasure in the feeling of existence will develop "a will to exist" and so, at least as we see it in humans, "a will to live." But I must unpack this. How does a *will* to exist differ from simply an *instinct* to exist, or just existing? Most biological organisms evidently manage to live their lives just fine without having the will to do so. We would never attribute a will to live to an oak tree, an earthworm, or a butterfly. These organisms, when the need arises, act instinctively in a variety of preprogrammed life-preserving ways. Human beings do the same much of the time. You eat your food, withdraw your hand from the flame, heal your wounds, and so on, without giving a thought to your existence. So how might there be added value in your having evolved to be *conscious* of existing?

It could work like this. If natural selection can arrange that you enjoy the feeling of existing, then existence can and does become a goal: something—indeed, as we'll see, some *thing*—you *want*. And the difference between your *wanting* to exist and simply having some kind of life instinct is that, when you *want* something, you will tend to engage in rational actions—flexible, intelligent behavior—to achieve it. You will do things that are not rewarding in themselves but that are calculated (on some level) to deliver the goal. You may even do things that are punishing—including going through pain.

I admit this may sound like some sort of bootstrap operation, rather as if natural selection had designed a creature to take pleasure in the sound of its own heartbeat. But why not, if it works? We accept that Nature made sex pleasurable so as to encourage animals to take the steps that lead to sexual intercourse. Then why not make the feeling of existence magically delightful in order to encourage conscious creatures to do the things that lead to their existing?

For human beings, the case hardly needs making. Happily, we have all seen how it plays out in our own lives. "Where am I going?" the boy sings in A. A. Milne's poem "Spring Morning":

> Where am I going? I don't quite know.
> Down to the stream where the king-cups grow—
> . . . .
> Where am I going? The high rooks call:
> "It's awful fun to be born at all."[12]

Awful fun is not the half of it. We know life can at times be unspeakably beautiful. But what about those high rooks? And galahs, and chimpanzees? Do nonhuman animals really *want to feel that they exist*? And if they do, is it indeed evidence that these animals are phenomenally conscious?

We need not doubt that there are many species of animals who, just like humans, go out of their way to have fun. They want, as it were, to live it up. The galahs seek out the whirl-winds. Dolphins follow a ship to ride the bow waves. Chimps beg to be tickled.

I once observed a young mountain gorilla who climbed a high vine to fetch down a gourd-like fruit. My field notes record: "She plays with the fruit, tossing it from side to side, letting it drop into her hands, then she grips the stalk between her teeth so that the fruit dangles from her mouth, stands bipedally and turns somersaults. Next she stands, still holding the fruit between her teeth, and beats it repeatedly with both hands, making a sharp clapping sound." The following day she came back to the same vine with the obvious intention of fetching down another so satisfactory a plaything.[13]

Every dog owner has seen the lengths to which a dog will go to get taken for a walk, the anticipatory joy when he succeeds, and the hang-dog look if he realizes he is not getting what he wants. There are few sights so pathetic as a dog who, having been taken out in the car for what might have been a run in the woods, realizes he is approaching a boarding kennel, where his existence will be put on hold.

Do examples such as these really add up to a will to exist in these animals? Certainly, if you were in their place, conscious presence would be both the goal and the condition of your making these efforts to engage with life. It would be the qualia you would be deliberately seeking. If you were a psychological zombie, you simply would not bother to do these things. And I would say it is a fair assumption (though by no means a logically secure one) that if the animals were zombies, they would not bother either. True, we should be cautious about reading too much into the behavior of species distant from ourselves. Yet we should not feel bound to read too little either.

▪ The survival benefits of delighting in "existence" are obvious. For a start, any creature who has it as a goal to indulge its senses in the kinds of ways described will be likely to engage in a range of activities that promote its bodily and mental well-being (even if occasionally at some risk). Such a creature will *do life* well, we might say. But it will not stop there. Since you can reach these moments of intense existence only by doing all the other things required to stay alive, then, for at least some animals, *being alive as such* will become a goal. You will not just live well, you will *want a life* because you *want to feel*.

So here is the crucial question. Could not natural selection have achieved the same result in easier ways? Given that there are indeed benefits to be had when living it up becomes a goal of behavior, then why not simply add some extra reward circuits to the brain so as to make the experience of intense and varied sensory stimulation "positively reinforcing," as the behaviorists would say, without going the extra mile to invent the drama of phenomenal consciousness? Psychological zombies could surely have sensory fun—of a zombie sort. Zombies could still be designed to engage in play.

Yes, so they could. But I believe the reason their play would be so much shallower—and in the long run less life affirming—than that of a conscious creature is this: phenomenal consciousness gives you (or at any rate gives you the illusion of) a *substantial thing* to value. The great object of life—the ball that, as a conscious being, you strive to keep in the air—is not a shallow physiological variable, not a mere number, but something psychologically in a different league. It is the existence of a *conscious self*.

There, I have said it: a "conscious self." It is time to bring the "self" to center stage. The concept of self is a complex one, and it will not be until much later in the book that we get the measure of it. I will argue later that in the course of evolutionary history, selves have come to exist on different levels in different species. The self of an adult human being certainly has no equivalent in animals (or human infants, for that matter).

But, to begin with, I want to focus on something basic: let's call it the "core self," by which I mean no more or less than *the owner and occupier of the thick moment of consciousness*. When "you feel that *you* exist" as the subject of sensation, the core self comes into existence in that illusory time space.

This is not my idea. It is originally Aristotle's idea (although seldom acknowledged as such in contemporary philosophy.) I wrote above, in chapter 4, how Aristotle drew attention to the paradoxical temporal depth of consciousness. "The undivided 'now' of sensation must rest upon a duration with which it does not altogether coincide. . . . It is another time . . . it may well be something other than any time at all." But where did he go with this? Remarkably, he went on to argue that it is precisely this "extra" time dimension that underlies—and brings into being—the core self: "If someone senses himself or something else in a continuous time, then it is impossible for him not to notice he exists. . . . In all sensation, simple or complex, sharp or dull, the animal . . . feels that it lives."[14]

Aristotle realized that it is impossible not to notice that *I am when I feel—Sentio ergo sum*. Descartes, fifteen hundred years later, claimed that it is impossible to doubt that *I am when I think—Cogito ergo sum*. Yet, as several modern writers have observed, Aristotle's "Sentio" is much truer to lived experience than Descartes' "Cogito." "Sometimes I think and other times I am," wrote the poet Paul Valéry.[15] For novelist Milan Kundera, "*I think, therefore I am* is the statement of an intellectual who underrates toothaches. *I feel, therefore I am* is a truth much more universally valid, and it applies to everything that's alive."[16]

The logical corollary of this, and indeed the obvious psychological fact, is that *if I do not feel, I am not*. Your core self comes into being only as and when you have sensations. And to suggest, as some theorists have, that there could already be the shell of a self—an empty self, waiting in the wings—ready to lay claim to sensations if and when they arise, is to get things back to front. The philosopher Gottlob Frege misleadingly argued that "an experience is impossible without an experiencer. The inner world presupposes the person whose inner world it is."[17] But in truth an experiencer is impossible without experience; the existence of the person presupposes the inner world that makes him who he is. Johann Fichte said it better: "What was I before I came to self-consciousness? The natural answer to this question is: I did not exist at all, for I was not an I."[18]

In fact, as natural historians of consciousness, this is something we see for ourselves every morning. At the beginning of this book I invoked the great awakening that happens each day on Earth: innumerable conscious selves emerging from the chrysalis of sleep. Marcel Proust wrote of how, on waking, there is "a rope let down from heaven to draw me up out of the abyss of not-being."[19] Here is Paul Valéry again: "One should not say *I* wake but There is waking—for the *I* is the result, the end, the ultimate Q.E.D."[20]

So then what next? What when, as the great physiologist Charles Sherrington has described it, "the full panel of the 'five-senses' is in session, and . . . the individual has attained a psychical existence"? From that moment on the core self becomes the entity that you, as a conscious creature, think of yourself *as being* and in whose future you now have a unique and peculiar interest. "Each waking day is a stage dominated for good or ill, in comedy, farce or tragedy, by a *dramatis persona*, the 'self.'"[21]

It is your own self, occupying *your* inner space. For let us note (and we will discuss this more fully later on) that it is a key feature of the self that emerges from sensation that it belongs to you, the subject, *alone*. Imagine how it would be if the "my space" of the social Internet were not only a Web site to which you were alone in having the password for uploading new information, but a site that was essentially unviewable by anyone else, and yet the site where it felt the real you resided. Imagine it? But that is precisely how it is! Your self has become essentially *your concern*, your responsibility.

Admittedly, there has been fierce debate among philosophers about whether this notion of the singular all-important self can stand up to analysis. Several critics have argued that people *ought not* to be so impressed by the autochthonous illusion of selfhood, as undoubtedly they mostly are. Thomas Metzinger wrote in response to an earlier essay of mine: "Of course no such things as selves exist in the world: nobody ever was or had a self. A self could never be something you have— like a bicycle or book by Dostoevsky. . . . The phenomenal self is not a thing, but a process."[22]

James Branch Cabell, the early twentieth-century American author and wit, took a particularly sardonic view of the importance people attach to this supposed *thing*: "What thing is it to which I so glibly refer as I? If you will try to form a notion of yourself, of the sort of a something that you suspect to inhabit and partially to control your flesh and blood body, you will [find] . . . there seems to remain in those pearl-colored brain-cells, wherein is your ultimate lair, very little save a faculty for receiving sensations. . . . And surely, to be just a very gullible consciousness provisionally existing among inexplicable mysteries, is not an enviable plight." "And yet," he added, "this life—to which I cling tenaciously—comes to no more."[23]

Maybe so. Yet, in light of our discussion, it seems obvious that these deconstructionists have missed the point: the point of what a self amounts to *psychologically*. Cabell, rather than ending on that downbeat note, might better have stressed the extraordinarily positive fact: "And yet, to this life—which comes to no more—I cling tenaciously." For it is *this* that matters: "the sort of a something," which as scientists we may well agree is "very little save a faculty for receiving sensations," has been transformed by the magic of conscious phenomenology into some *thing* that you can cling to. The great object in life has become that your core self should thrive. As William James wrote: "To have a self that I can *care for*, nature must first present me with some *object* interesting enough to make me instinctively wish to appropriate it for its *own* sake."[24]

We can only guess how wide the circle goes among non-human animals—how wide the charmed circle of those who *because they live in the conscious present* can contemplate and enjoy their own existence. To declare my prejudice, I do not think that gnats—even joyful, dancing gnats—have a will to exist or have so much as a smidgen of a conscious self. I have no opinion about fish and cold-blooded land vertebrates. But I do take seriously the evidence for mammals and birds. What I see there—in a cat's and gorilla's and panda's and galah's straining for sensation—are indeed the signs of a core self devoted to its own continuance.

But we cannot leave things at this point, with consciousness simply as a motive to *love life* in certain species, including our own. As natural historians, we have to see the extra face of this. For there is at least one species of animal for which clinging to life tenaciously means more than loving life. With human beings, it also means *fearing personal death*—the extinction of the self. This will loom still larger for us toward the end of the book. But some of the issues are pressing, and I want to go there right away.

Though we have been discussing the evolution of consciousness in animals in general, we have every reason to be especially interested in human beings. And when the evidence suggests that there is something special going on with humans, we must not ignore it. As it happens, all the issues raised earlier in this chapter about the motivating effects of consciousness as a biological force come into sharpest focus when we consider an outcome that very likely matters to human beings alone.

Human *beings*. It could hardly be more obvious. *Being* is what it is all about. But this creates problems for humans of a unique kind. Humans are a part of nature, yet in one respect they are at a disadvantage to all other species. They know too much. They want to *be*, yet they know that every precedent—all too well recorded—teaches that *not being* is their certain fate. John Keats was twenty-four years old when he enjoyed that nectarine, but within two years he had died from consumption in Rome. Rupert Brooke was twenty-seven when he wrote that poem, "The Great Lover," and a year later he succumbed to septicemia on a troopship in the Dardanelles. Albert Camus was forty-six when, with the unfinished manuscript of his story of growing up in Algeria in a bag beside him, he was killed in a car crash on the road to Paris.

Inevitably, you see that it is coming your way too. Yet, being no less in love with life than any other conscious creature, your own death may seem completely out of order—it was never part of the deal. Tom Nagel has said it well: "Observed from without, human beings obviously have a natural lifespan and cannot live much longer than a hundred years. A man's sense of his own experience, on the other hand, does not embody this idea of a natural limit. His existence defines for him an essentially open-ended possible future, containing the usual mixture of goods and evils that he has found so tolerable in the past. . . . Viewed in this way, death, no matter how inevitable, is an abrupt cancellation of indefinitely extensive possible goods."[25]

You signed up to *be there indefinitely*. And maybe nothing hits you harder than the realization that one day you will not be able to. Here is an excerpt from an interview with the novelist Philip Roth. "'You said you're afraid of dying. You're 72. What are you afraid of?' He looks at me. 'Oblivion. Of not being alive, quite simply, of not feeling life, not smelling it.'"[26]

True, it can be argued that to be afraid of oblivion is a kind of logical error: you cannot reasonably fear not feeling, because not feeling is not a state of being. Two thousand years ago the poet Lucretius tried to persuade us that after we die, "we shall not feel, because we shall not Be. . . . And since the Man who *Is* not feels not woe (For death exempts him and wards off the blow, which we, the living, only feel and bear), What is there left for us in Death to fear?"[27]

We may agree that, strictly speaking, oblivion is unimaginable because the mind cannot simulate a state of mindlessness.[28] But that is hardly the point. When you fear death, it is not that you fear being somewhere you cannot imagine, it is that you fear *not being* somewhere you *can imagine* (and are living in right now). Philip Larkin made the argument better than anyone in his poem "Aubade." "Specious stuff," he calls it,

> . . . that says no rational being
> Can fear a thing it cannot feel, not seeing
> That this is what we fear—no sight, no sound,
> No touch or taste or smell, nothing to think with,
> Nothing to love or link with,
> The anaesthetic from which none come round.[29]

The point is that oblivion figures in people's imagination as the *negation* of being there. You fear the deletion of "my space"—as Nagel said, the *cancellation* of possible goods. Zombies would have nothing to worry about even if they saw death coming, because they could not fear the absence of something they have never had. Humans, however, can and do fear death precisely because of what they do have.

It means that for human beings, this fear is indeed one of the *public effects of consciousness*: something that would surely catch the attention of the Andromedan scientist if she were looking. It is a big effect too. The psychoanalyst Ernest Becker has written: "The idea of death, the fear of it, haunts the human animal like nothing else; it is the mainspring of human activity—activity designed largely to avoid the fatality of death, to overcome it by denying in some way that it is the final destiny of man."[30] To the extent that this is true, it follows that human beings' fear of death must always have been highly visible to natural selection—and hence so must have been the consciousness that lies behind it.

As we will see later in the book, anxieties about death show up in human behavior at many different levels and have been a driving force in the development of culture and civilization. But for now I want to keep the discussion simple. Does the raw fear of oblivion help people survive?

I have not seen the question put like this before. But maybe that is because the answer is so obvious. Jean-Jacques Rousseau may have exaggerated when he claimed, "Without [the fear of dying,] the entire human species would soon be destroyed."[31] But it is certainly the case that in a thousand different circumstances, human beings have looked death in the face and—not liking what they saw—have taken whatever steps they could to avoid it.

Let's take just one example. The climber Joe Simpson, in his astonishing tale of survival after a climbing accident in the Andes, *Touching the Void,* relates how, first of all, the feeling of pain reassured him: "A burning, searing agony reached up from my leg. It was bent beneath me. As the burning increased so the sense of living became fact. Heck! I couldn't be dead and feel that! It kept burning, and I laughed—Alive! Well fuck me!—and laughed again, a real happy laugh."[32] That night, Simpson found Shakespeare's lines running through his head, teasing him, urging him on:

The weariest and most loathed worldly life
That age, ache, penury, and imprisonment
Can lay on nature, is a paradise
To what we fear of death.[33]

The *void:* Simpson touched it and recoiled. And so he dragged himself back into the world of the living.

Presumably there have been countless other instances where humans have done the same—refused to succumb because they were not ready to let go, because, in the words of Dylan Thomas, they "raged against the dying of the light,"[34] not of course always with such admirable acts of courage. To avoid personal death, people will sometimes behave in craven and immoral self-serving ways. As Dr. Johnson famously said: "Depend upon it, sir, when a man knows he is to be hanged in a fortnight, it concentrates his mind wonderfully."[35] And when he knows he will be dead in the next hour, unless he does something about it, we should not be surprised if his mind turns to escape, perhaps at any cost. Modern humans are not necessarily the descendants of heroes; they are the descendants of those who stayed alive when others did not. Like it or not, human consciousness must regularly have proved its biological worth in just such moments of last resort.

Think of the extravagant lengths to which throughout history people have been prepared to go in the vain hope of ensuring the survival of their selves *after* they die. How much more have they always invested in not dying to start with.

■ But these are indeed human responses. Do any nonhuman animals fear death? It has generally been assumed that they do not—actually *could* not. I do not disagree. There are three reasons for saying so.

The first is that nonhuman animals have a limited capacity for "mental time travel."[36] Even if they are able to look forward to the future, and to imagine the possible recurrence of good or bad things that have happened in the past, it is very unlikely that they can imagine a *hypothetical* scenario: the occurrence of something that has never yet happened to them. Yet dying is of course just that—a lifetime first. It means a nonhuman animal could not think about being hanged in ten minutes' time, let alone a fortnight. As W. H. Auden wrote, contrasting this state of blissful ignorance starkly with that of humans: "Happy the hare at morning, for she cannot read / The Hunter's waking thoughts. Lucky the leaf / Unable to predict the fall."[37]

The second reason is that nonhuman animals will not have had anything like the exposure that humans have to the accumulated evidence of death. Even if an animal has had occasion to see another animal die, it will still not have much cause to generalize this fate to include itself, let alone see death of some sort as inevitable. Voltaire remarked: "The human race is the only one that knows it must die, and it knows this only through its experience. A child brought up alone and transported to a desert island would have no more idea of death than a cat or a plant."[38] It may be true that if an animal has seen another of its species killed, after being caught by a lion, for example, then, provided it is clever enough, it might possibly conclude that if it itself gets caught by a lion, it will be killed too. But without the support of a shared culture, this is a lesson very unlikely to be learned.

But the third and clinching reason is that nonhuman animals do not have the conceptual wherewithal to appreciate the finality of death. How could the animal possibly anticipate that the death of the body brings with it the death of the self? If an animal thinks about it at all, it will most likely conflate being dead with being asleep. And sleep, though it does entail the temporary extinction of consciousness, is of course

Being There

not such a disaster. Indeed, everyone's experience—yours too—has been that sleep is a bourn from which the self has always returned. This is no doubt why human beings find sleep such a seductive model for being dead. And if humans do not always get the truth of it, is it likely that nonhumans ever do?

The difficulties that chimpanzees have in appreciating that death is the end is revealed in the primatologist Tetsuro Matsuzawa's observations of a group of wild chimpanzees at Bossou, Guinea, following the death from pneumonia of a two-and-a-half-year-old female infant, Jokro.[39] I quote Matsuzawa's field notes verbatim (a marvelous film is also available online):

> January 25th 1992.
> Jire [Jokro's mother] puts her daughter on the ground.
> I look at Jokro's chest, but see no signs of breathing.
> I realize that she is dead—she died this very day. Jire
> takes Jokro's hand and places her body on her back.
> Just like when she was alive, Jokro is "riding" on her
> mother's back in prone posture.

> January 27th.
> Two days have passed since Jokro's death. Her corpse
> is lying face up, supine posture, on the back of the
> mother. The belly is swollen with gas. Jokro's body has
> started to decompose. Jire chases away the flies circling
> her dead infant.

> January 29th.
> 4 days after death, Jokro's body has begun to dry out—
> it is mummifying. But the mother has returned to

carrying it the way she would a live infant—right side up, and in the normal prone position. Tua, the alpha male of the community, sniffs Jokro's corpse. I myself can smell the strong odour of decomposition. However, other members of the community show no signs of aversion to or fear of the lifeless body.

February 9th.
15 days have passed since Jokro died. Her body has now completely dried out. Jire continues to chase away the flies attracted to the dead body. Then, she picks up the body and looks directly into its face. She starts to clean Jokro's face. She grooms her daughter's remains as if she were still alive. Soon after, I observe a youngster playing with the body, while the adults are taking a rest. He takes Jokro's body and climbs a tree with it. He swings the corpse and lets it fall to the ground from a height of about 5 metres. He rushes down the tree and picks it up, then climbs up and drops it again. Meanwhile, Jire looks on gently.

February 17th.
A very interesting episode occurs. Tua, the alpha male of the community, rushes toward me in a charging display. He uses Jokro's mummified body as a part of his display. Chimpanzees usually use dead branches to accentuate power in a charging display. Yet this time, Tua uses the body of a dead infant. However, I notice a subtle detail. When Tua turns around, he gently switches the body from his right to left hand. With

branches, he has never shown such delicate handling as with Jokro's remains. Tua abandons the body right in front of me. The mother, Jire, retrieves Jokro's body, just as she always has.

If chimpanzees find it so hard to appreciate what has happened when, in front of their eyes, one of their number has permanently ceased to be alive, we can be sure that this is not a fate that they can ever imagine to be coming their own way. And if they cannot imagine it, they cannot fear it.

I argued earlier that there are many nonhuman animals that, because they value their own consciousness, *enjoy life* and *want* more of it. And chimpanzees are of course up among the best of them. "The creature . . . will *want to live* because it *wants to feel*." My point now is that if you are a nonhuman animal, you can very well want to live without having any fear of death, given that either you do not see it coming or do not understand that death means no more life. It is these dreadful premonitions that make the human situation so much more anxiety laden—but also, for that very reason, so much more focused on survival.

■ We are at a surprising pass. If fearing death is, indeed, a uniquely human trait, if fearing death is one of the consequences of being conscious, and if fearing death helps to keep human beings alive, this suggests that consciousness—core consciousness—contributes more to the biological fitness of human beings than to that of any other animal. It could even mean that human consciousness, at this basic core level, has in fact come under new pressure from natural selection.

We might have expected that new kinds of selection pressure would be in play when it comes to the grander forms of selfhood that I will discuss later in the book. But I think no one—unless he or she had independently made the journey of this chapter—would have expected this in relation to the core self. Whether this has really made a significant contribution to the phenomenology of consciousness in humans—whether it has reshaped the ipsundrum—is a tantalizing question. But, as I said, we should delay discussion of all such issues about the possibility of there being species differences in "what it is like" to be phenomenally aware until we have a more complete picture of how consciousness may have developed to serve this role and others.

Let's move on then to another, very different way in which the internal magic show can change your life: by having you cast a spell beyond your own body on your physical surroundings.

7   The Enchanted World

You feel life, smell it. Your own existence can at times be all absorbing. "Everything seems futile here except the sun, our kisses, and the wild scents of the earth." In such a state of body-centered reverie, phenomenal consciousness might seem to be about nothing but *being me*. The sensations you yourself are staging occupy your mind, and you give no thought to the *things in the outside world* to which they answer. In fact, when basking in the present moment, you may want to pull away from the world altogether.

I promised to take evidence about the natural history of consciousness from artists and monks. So let us acknowledge that there are traditions of art and traditions of religious meditation that, while celebrating the conscious present, make a point of leaving *worldly things* out of the picture altogether.

Bridget Riley writes: "If I am outside in nature, I do not look for something or at things. I try to absorb sensations without censoring them, without identifying them. I want them to come through the pores of my eyes, as it were—on a particular level of their own."[1] And the finished work of art has to be appreciated as pure sensation too. Paul Cézanne tells us: "Shut your eyes, wait, think of nothing. Now open them. . . . One sees nothing but a great coloured undulation. What then? An irradiation and glory of colour. That is what a picture should give us, a warm harmony, an abyss in which the evil eye is lost, a secret germination, a coloured state of grace."[2] Henri Matisse, in a famous painting now in the New York Museum of Modern Art, made a copy of a still life by Jan de Heem in which, following Cézanne's advice, he pointedly went against the original artist's intention and instead represented a sumptuous banquet as a flat arrangement of colored forms.

Kandinsky, as we saw in chapter 2, urged a musical analogy: "Color is the keyboard, the eyes are the hammers, the soul is the piano with many strings." Walter Pater claimed that "all art constantly aspires to the condition of music."[3] So let us remark that music can lift you into a state of self-absorbed detachment from the world more effectively than any other artistic medium. Perhaps this is just because, in listening to music, you can so easily cease to pay attention to where the music comes from, that is, easily hear it as *sound at your ear* rather than as *the sound of something out there in the world*.

"Is it not strange that sheeps' guts should hale souls out of men's bodies?" asks Benedick in *Much Ado about Nothing*.[4] Yet, if this does strike you as strange, it is surely because this is really *not the way you hear it*: when your soul is haled by the music of the lute, you can—and often will—remain gloriously uninterested in the vibrations of the gut string stretched across the wooden box. We say that you may "lose yourself" in listening to music. Yet it might be closer to the truth to say that you lose the world and find more of your core self.

However, there is another side to it. Being conscious is not only about being your self. As we are about to see—arguably, as natural selection was about to see—phenomenal consciousness also profoundly changes your relationship to the external world.

■ I assume you recognize and value the state of detached self-absorption just described. Still, I assume too that this state is relatively unusual. In fact, more commonly, even while you are aware of your own existence, you are nonetheless keenly aware of the existence of things in your environment.

When you are outside in nature, unlike Riley, you *do* look for something and at things—you identify and celebrate, say, the mountain and the tree for what they are. Even when you listen to the sounds of music, unlike Benedick, you can and sometimes will listen to the clash of the cymbal, the twang of the cello string as such. And these *outward-directed* states are not necessarily states of lesser consciousness. Far from it; I would say they may be states in which phenomenal consciousness is asserting itself more strongly than ever.

We can take evidence on this side too. There are indeed other traditions of painting and other traditions of meditation that teach the path of living as attentively as possible in and among things.

Matisse transformed the banqueting table into "a great colored undulation." But in the original painting, De Heem depicted fat grapes, a glittering decanter, a game pie, white

linen, crystal goblets, deep velvet cloth, and a polished man-
dolin, with every detail lovingly modeled. His intention was
not just to create a feast for the eyes, but to draw attention to
the glories of the world in *its own right*.

In a Christian cathedral you may be transported heaven-
ward, but in a Zen garden you are pointedly returned to earth.
In the garden your existence is not primary: the lesson is that
you exist alongside other existents—the rocks, the water, the
golden carp, and the rooted cedar.

In chapter 6 I quoted many examples of people and animals taking pleasure, as I put it, in "pure being." Yet let's recognize now that even in cases where selfhood may have been very
much the focus, there has been more going on. Keats certainly
reveled in the oozy, slushy sweet sensations, but surely he also
enjoyed *the nectarine as such*. The chimpanzee Gaia reveled in
the cool water swirling around her fingers, but surely she also
delighted in the existence of the stream.

And Brooke? His poem continues:

Sweet water's dimpling laugh from tap or spring;
Holes in the ground; and voices that do sing;
Voices in laughter, too; and body's pain,
Soon turned to peace; and the deep-panting train;
Firm sands; the little dulling edge of foam
That browns and dwindles as the wave goes home;
And washen stones, gay for an hour; the cold
Graveness of iron; moist black earthen mould;
Sleep; and high places; footprints in the dew;
And oaks; and brown horse-chestnuts, glossy-new;
And new-peeled sticks; and shining pools on grass.

The poet is pinpointing his personal sensory pleasures. Yet clearly he is also in awe of the source of these pleasures out there in the world. Things. Plain old things, and so many of them. Things that, for the most part, are of no earthly use to human beings—no good for eating or selling or making love to. Things, it might seem, that have little if, anything, to do with a human life. But things whose simple *factuality* is a cause for feeling glad.

> Glory be to God for dappled things—
> For skies of couple-colour as a brinded cow;
> For rose-moles all in stipple upon trout that swim;
> Fresh-firecoal chestnut-falls; finches' wings. . . .[5]

Gerard Manley Hopkins, like Brooke, multiplies examples to drive home the message. It is as if, in the manner of the Dutch still-life painters, these writers want to showcase the world's bounty, to pile the table with riches, so as to prove our good fortune in living in this world where each and every object calls out to be adored because of its intrinsic value.

But we have no need to rely on high poetry to make the point. Popular culture has its own way of saying it. "These I have loved," writes Brooke. "These are a few of my favourite things," sings Maria in *The Sound of Music*.[6]

> Raindrops on roses and whiskers on kittens
> Bright copper kettles and warm woolen mittens
> Brown paper packages tied up with strings.

She is not finished. And it would seem almost loutish to break in to ask what is going on here. Yet the question is pressing: how can we explain this adoration for things as such?

Cream coloured ponies and crisp apple strudels
Doorbells and sleigh bells and schnitzel with noodles
Wild geese that fly with the moon on their wings
· ·
Girls in white dresses with blue satin sashes
Snowflakes that stay on my nose and eyelashes
Silver white winters that melt into springs
These are a few of my favorite things.

What role, if any, should we assign to consciousness in this? Could it even be that only a creature who is personally conscious will mind so much about *impersonal facts*? You might think this a surprising possibility. Then prepare to be very surprised.

■ Let us start by raising the obvious question with regard to consciousness and things. Would a psychological zombie find the outside world so full of wonders?

The question is not, whether a zombie would have his own list of favorites. Of course he would. Presumably, a zombie, even if he lacks sensory qualia, should still be perfectly capable of evaluating things in his environment as good or bad for him, especially when it concerns his bodily functions. A zombie, presumably, would know what he likes. Thus we might well expect to find him listing among his favorites such good-for-the body items as, for example, warm woolen mittens and crisp apple strudels.

But the question, rather, is, whether a zombie's list of favorites would be *nearly as long* as that of a typical conscious human being. And I think the answer is that his list would be *nothing as long,* for two reasons, both of which have to do with consciousness. One reason is relatively straightforward, arising from issues we have already discussed; the second is more unexpected.

A few lines back I wrote that you as a normal human being love things that are of no use to you. However, if we look at the lists again, it is obvious that many of the things you love, even if "useless," tickle your senses in just such a way as to contribute to your feeling of living in the present and having a core self—which is indeed partly why you love them. So, the straightforward reason why a zombie's list of favorites would be shorter than yours is simply that, since a zombie does not have a conscious present to live in, he would not include *those* items on his list. Therefore, notably missing from the zombie's list would be such purely good-for-the-soul thick-moment-filling items as, for example, holes in the ground, newly peeled sticks, finches' wings, and brown paper parcels tied up with string.

Yet this cannot be the whole story, for it would imply that the love of things is really just more of the same: the love of self (and whatever helps sustain it). However, as we have seen in the many examples I have cited just now, people again and again profess to love things in their own right.

Imagine yourself walking in the woods after the rain: sunshine filters through the dripping leaves, a song thrush sings, and the scent of primroses permeates the rich air. No doubt you feel it is good to be *you* in this world of sights and sounds and smells. But at the same time, do you also not feel it is good for the *primrose to be yellow*, and the *leaves to be wet*, and the *thrush to be trilling*? In fact, is it not true that your dominant feeling toward the things you are interacting with is not of gratitude for a service provided (though there is that too) but of wonder that such things exist as what they are? Dare I suggest that, strangely enough, you love the things for being the things they are *almost* in the same way that you love yourself for being your self?

So what is going on? I want to describe it as follows. It is as if, when you see and hear and touch and taste things, some of the magic of your phenomenal sensation is rubbing off onto the things as such. And this has the extraordinary result of making it seem to you as if *the things themselves possess phenomenal qualities*. As if things out there in the world have an extra dimension of subjective *presence*. Maybe even as if *you have a private line to them*, as if they are imbued with *your subjectivity*.

But of course none of this makes sense! We have established in the first chapters of the book that the phenomenal properties of sensation are the properties of a very special kind of activity *you are creating* inside your head. What is more, they are illusory, "impossible" properties. There is therefore no way that these properties can be properties of things out there in the world. Why, then, should you even begin to think that way?

▨ Let's return to the discussion of sensation and sentition. In figure 5, I illustrated the situation when someone looks, for example, at a red tomato. The explanation of this figure reads: "Red light arrives at your eyes, and you create an internalized expressive response, you engage in redding. You monitor what you are doing so as to discover what is happening to you. And the representation you form of your own response is the sensation of red." To say it again: it is *your* show, you are creating the ipsundrum with its phenomenal properties as your way of representing the stimulation at your body surface and how you feel about it. The red tomato skin is indeed responsible for the stimulation. But objectively, there is nothing illusion-generating or phenomenal about the tomato as such.

The Enchanted World

So, if now you do in fact believe that the phenomenal properties *inhere in the external thing as such*, this can be only because you are somehow *projecting the sensation out of your own head into the world.*[7] In figure 10 I have tried to illustrate what seems to be occurring. But I expect this illustration makes it only all the more obvious how anomalous such "projection" is. What exactly does "projecting sensation" amount to? Does it mean that the phenomenal properties of your sensation now pertain to an entity that is *not you*? The answer, I suggest, is both yes and no. That is, what is happening is that you do still feel yourself involved, even *bodily* involved, in the sensation, only the limits of your body have mysteriously been spread out to coincide with the distal world.

I hope I can explain better what this means by referring to a remarkable experimental demonstration.[8] In an experiment by Carrie Armel and V. S. Ramachandran, a subject (S) sits at a table with his hand hidden from view by a partition (P),

Figure 10.
How sensation gets "projected": the subjective quality of redness moves over and becomes attached to the perceived external object.

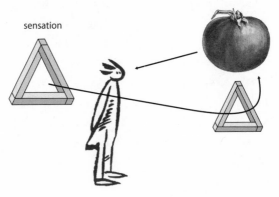

sensation

while there is a fake rubber hand (FH) in full view in front of him (see figure 11, top). His own hand and the rubber hand are then tapped and stroked in synchrony by the experimenter (E). It turns out that in this situation, the subject unexpectedly reports that he feels the corresponding tactile sensations to be located *where the rubber hand is*.

But wait. If there is no rubber hand in view and the real hand and *a spot on the tabletop* are tapped and stroked in synchrony (figure 11, bottom), the subject now says he feels the sensation to be located at that *spot in the table*. What is more,

Figure 11.

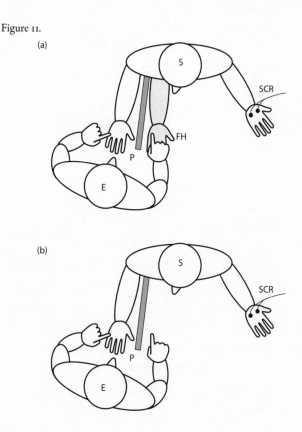

(a)

(b)

when a Band-Aid is placed on both the real hand and the spot on the table, and then the Band-Aid is suddenly ripped off the table, the subject shows an emotional change in skin conductance as if expecting pain.[9]

This finding, it must be said, was unanticipated. But the experimenters were able to provide a ready explanation. In their paper they suggest that the illusion occurs because the subject is seeking the statistically most probable way of integrating what he or she is seeing and feeling. If you feel a particular pattern of tactile sensation in the skin of your hand and see a highly correlated pattern of stroking at a specific place in the external world, the most likely (even if erroneous) inference will be that there is only *one* event rather than *two*—so that the tactile sensation must be located where the stroking is seen to be occurring.

Armel and Ramachandran do indeed title their paper "Projecting Sensations to External Objects." But, to return to the question of what's meant by "projection," let's note that, in the first instance, you, the subject, will not conclude it is *the table* that is having the tactile sensation; rather, it is *you* who are having the sensation *in the skin of your hand, which has moved onto the table.*

You may well think this is an odd way for things to turn out. But it becomes odder still. For if the tabletop has *become the skin of your hand,* then, while you still feel the tactile sensation to be a representation of what is happening to *you,* two things follow. First, it will seem that *the table as such is sensitive to touch.* Second, it will seem that what's happening to the table when it is touched has *phenomenal qualities*—as if the table is doing something in response to stimulation *on a level with sentition,* as if the table is itching or paining!

Chapter 7

The experimenters were as surprised as anyone.[10] "To our astonishment," they write, "subjects often reported sensations arising from the table surface, despite the fact that it bears no visual resemblance to a hand." They then ask, only half jokingly, "If you looked through a telescope at the moon and used an optical trick to stroke and touch it in synchrony with your hand, would you 'project' the sensations to the moon?"

They do not answer their own question. But I would say it is a perfectly reasonable and pertinent question, and one that would be more pertinent still if we were to ask it not about touch but about *vision*. If you looked at the moon and saw that its surface was being "touched by light" in synchrony with light arriving at your own eye, would you project your *visual sensation* to the moon?

But while we are at it, why don't we ask the same question about the case of looking at a red tomato? Suppose we substitute the "skin of the eye" (which is to say, the retina at the back of the eyeball) for the skin of the hand, the "touch of light" for the stroke of the experimenter, and the tomato for the table. Then, I think, the logic of the situation should be very similar. And to make it more similar still, why don't we imagine that the tomato, rather than being constantly illuminated, is being stroked with the light of a flashlight? In this case, here is how the argument, transposed from tactile to visual sensation, would go.[11]

When you look at the tomato being stroked by the flashlight, you sense a particular spatiotemporal pattern of light at your eye, and at the same time you perceive a highly correlated pattern of events occurring out there at the tomato. Just as with the table, then, you will make the inference that in all probability these two events are one, so that the visual sensation must be located where the light is falling. Again you will not, in the first instance, conclude that the tomato is having the visual sensation; rather, it is *you* who are having the sensation *in a part of the skin of your eye which now seems to coincide with the skin of the tomato.* However, if the tomato has *become part of the skin of your eye,* while you still feel the visual sensation to be a representation of what is happening to you, two things follow, as before. First, it will seem that the *tomato as such is sensitive to light.* Second, it will seem that what happens to the tomato when light falls on it has *phenomenal* qualities—as if the tomato is redding!

I realize, of course, you yourself would not analyze it in this way, and you might want to use different words if you use words at all. Yet, I believe we have here the complete explanation for the effect I was struggling to find words for above: "the magic of your phenomenal sensation is rubbing off onto the things as such." And the story holds not just for red tomatoes and ticklish tables but across the entire range of your sensory and perceptual interaction with the world. At every opportunity you find yourself projecting your own phenomenal experience out into the world of things. Or rather, I should say, you do not *find yourself* doing this except when, as with the table, the result seems so bizarre: most of the time you never notice your own role in giving things their marvelous qualities—you simply assume that is the way they are made.

True, logically speaking, it does not make sense. The attribution of these phenomenal qualities to impersonal things really is a *category mistake*—a philosophical error where a property is being ascribed to a thing that could not possibly have that property. As the philosopher Thomas Reid sagely remarked more than two hundred years ago: "The confounding our sensations with that perception of external objects which is constantly conjoined with them, has been the occasion of most of the errors and false theories of philosophers with regard to the senses."[12]

If it is an error, however, is it one that you ought to regret? My answer, as I trust you will have seen by now, is no; quite the opposite. For it is precisely this misattribution of phenomenal qualities that gives conscious human beings the impression that they live surrounded by things of unaccountable loveliness in their own right. What matters is psychological impact, not philosophical rectitude. And, psychologically, the result is that you come to inhabit an enchanted world.

What would persuade you that it is indeed *you* who are the enchanter, *you* who are, as it were, coloring things with the fairy dust of your own consciousness? I would say that as compelling evidence as any comes from the reported effects of taking psychotropic drugs. Aldous Huxley vividly described his own experience with mescaline: "The books, for example, with which my study walls were lined. Like the flowers, they glowed, when I looked at them, with brighter colours, a profounder significance. Red books, like rubies; emerald books; books bound in white jade; books of agate; of aquamarine, of yellow topaz."[13] When the outside world takes on new qualities just as your personal sensation is intensified, there can be little doubt where the qualities are coming from: they have to be all a part of *your* show.

But there is a larger lesson to be drawn from such drug-induced experiences. The lesson is that no drugs are needed because what Huxley describes is clearly on a continuum with everyone's everyday experience. The fact is, wherever you, as a phenomenally conscious creature, cast your eye, ordinary things glow with bright colors and profound significance.

Borrowed phenomenality transforms the world into an awesome place. How often have you stared into a flaming fire, listened to the hoot of an owl in a dark wood, dangled your feet in a cold stream, or watched the sun setting in a blaze of color and been knocked back by the transcendent beauty of it? How often have you been captivated by some gemlike detail of your environment that seems almost too right and too good to be true, leaving you, perhaps, like Marcel Proust's Bergotte, in thrall to "the precious substance of the tiny patch of yellow wall"?[14]

"A beauty," Bergotte says, "that was sufficient in itself." "In itself," "as such," "in its own right"—these are indeed the phrases that come to mind. The impression you get that the qualities inhere in the things as such is, we have seen, all part of the illusion. But even as you celebrate the things for being themselves, it will not escape you that it is a peculiarly generous kind of self-sufficiency, where things are self-sufficient in ways that are the very qualities you care about. The things *are singing your song*.

No wonder that people sometimes lose track of who is the object and who the subject of this magical relationship. The Victorian artist William Rothenstein described how "one's very being seems to be absorbed into the fields, trees and the walls one is striving to paint. . . . At rare moments while painting I have felt myself caught, as it were, in a sort of cosmic rhythm."[15] For Vincent van Gogh, in the park in Arles, the experience of union was even more obviously one of interpenetration: "I have never had such a chance, nature here being so extraordinarily beautiful. Everywhere and all over the vault of heaven is a marvellous blue, and the sun sheds a radiance of pale sulphur, and it is soft and as lovely as the combination of heavenly blues and yellows in a Vermeer of Delft. . . . I am ravished with what I see. . . . I have a lover's insight or a lover's blindness."[16]

So, having reached these heights, dare we ask what is the *evolutionary story* behind this?

The caption to one of the illustrations in a recent book, *The Last Human*, reads: "The play of light and shadow between tree, sun and sky fills this Neanderthal man with a sense of awe."[17] Did ancestral humans really feel this way about the world and their relationship to it? Do any living nonhuman animals do so? The dog sits staring at the fire, as if entranced. The chimpanzee is mesmerized by the running stream. The infant gorilla is thrilled by the thump of the drum-fruit she discovers. Let me add a new example: dolphins have been seen to delight in blowing bubble rings in the water, playing with their creations, standing back, and relishing them, as if to say "See what I've got here."[18] We do not know. But I would say we should happily assume that, just to the extent that nonhuman creatures do experience phenomenal consciousness, they too are bound to end up making the same philosophical errors of attribution that modern human beings find so compelling. So, yes, Neanderthals almost certainly felt awe at the beauty of the world. On their own level, some nonhuman animals probably feel it too.

By the same token, we can say that a *psychological zombie would not feel it at all*. A zombie would never make the mistake of coloring the world with projected qualia or of misjudging his own boundaries and feeling himself mysteriously connected to nature. Indeed, imagine if you can the zombie's world. It would have to be a *disenchanted* world—a world where things no longer glow or have any phenomenal significance. The great psychologist William James raised that possibility as a dreadful thought experiment: "Conceive yourself, if possible, suddenly stripped of all the emotion of which your world now inspires you, and try to imagine it *as it exists*, purely by itself, without your favorable or unfavorable, hopeful or apprehensive comment. It will be almost impossible for you to realize such a condition of negativity and deadness."[19]

It sounds bad. We have said it before: *you do not want to be a zombie.* But now we have established a powerful extra reason, which is that for the zombie the world must be an infinitely drearier place. However, the evolutionary question is of course not settled by this. We need to ask whether a dreary world is necessarily one in which an animal or a human would lead a less successful life. We need to establish what, if any, is the biological advantage to being awestruck.

I admit we are so far from having any solid evidence about this—where is the natural history we need?—that we can only guess where the advantage may possibly lie. But at least we can guess as insiders (pity the Andromedan scientist who lacks our first-person take on it). So here goes.

I think, to start with, we can plausibly argue that some of the effects of enchanting the world will be of the very same kind as those we considered in the previous chapter: essentially a deepening of *joie de vivre*. If it is good to be alive, then it will be better still to be alive in a world where there is so much to enjoy. Robert Louis Stevenson said it so nicely in two lines of his *Child's Garden of Verses*: "The world is so full of a number of things, I'm sure we should all be as happy as Kings."[20] All the arguments deployed above about the benefits of desiring to *be there* will be reinforced when this desire is fed not just by love of self but by love of things outside.

But as insiders we can guess there will be more to it than this. For when it comes to it, it is not just about the joy of living but about the *point* of living too. How so? Because the externalization of value that results from projecting sensations onto objects—however philosophically tendentious—provides a whole new basis for believing that life has meaning. If it is good to be alive, then it is even better to be alive in *a good world*. George Santayana wrote: "That life is worth living is the most necessary of assumptions and, were it not assumed, the most impossible of conclusions."[21] I hesitate to contradict him outright about the impossibility of the conclusion. But I will gladly let Rupert Brooke—yes, Brooke again—do it for me, by pointing out how a love of things can seem to justify the lover's life.

When a friend wrote to Brooke to tell him he was overcome by pessimism, Brooke, just twenty-three years old, replied:

> I have a remedy. It is a dangerous one, but I think very
> good on the whole. . . . The remedy . . . consists in just
> looking at people and things as themselves—neither as
> useful nor moral nor ugly nor anything else; but just
> as being. . . . In a flicker of sunlight on a blank wall, or
> a reach of muddy pavement, or smoke from an engine
> at night, there's a sudden significance and importance
> and inspiration that makes the breath stop with a gulp
> of certainty and happiness. It's not that the wall or
> the smoke seem important for anything, or suddenly

reveal any general statement, or are rationally seen to be good or beautiful in themselves,—only that for you they're perfect and unique. It's like being in love with a person, . . . one is extraordinarily excited that the person, exactly as he is, uniquely and splendidly just exists. It's a feeling, not a belief. Only it's a feeling that has amazing results. I suppose my occupation is being in love with the universe. . . . With such superb work to do, and with the wild adventure of it all, and with the . . . enchantment of being even for a moment alive in a world of real matter . . . and actual people,—I have no time now to be a pessimist.[22]

If we want an additional adaptive function for consciousness, perhaps "being in love with the universe" will do!

But more specifically, what might this love affair translate into? The term "love" has figured repeatedly in the foregoing discussion. I would say we should take it seriously. Love is a powerful emotion. It motivates the lover to *engage with the objects of his love*—to seek them out, cherish them, and make more of them. And if he is in love with everything there is? Why, then he becomes a creature devoted to *play*, to *discovery* and *artistic creation*, inveterately curious.

In that same book, *The Last Human*, a caption to another illustration reads: "A juvenile *Australopithecus africanus* greets a new morning two and a half million years ago." We may well imagine the australopithecine child going out into the playground of the African savanna with the same joyous anticipation shown by the human child we saw celebrated in A. A. Milne's poem—a child whose enthusiasm for engaging with whatever comes his way is, we can now say, driven not just by the fun of feeling *he* exists, but the fun of discovering *what in the world* exists.

> If you were a bird, and lived on high,
> You'd lean on the wind when the wind came by,
> You'd say to the wind when it took you away:
> "*That's* where I wanted to go today!"

> Where am I going? I don't quite know.
> What does it matter where people go?
> Down to the wood where the blue-bells grow—
> Anywhere, anywhere. *I* don't know.[23]

The authors of a book about children's minds, which they title *The Scientist in the Crib,* write: "Human children in the first three years of life are consumed by a desire to explore and experiment with objects."[24] "Science", in the grand sense, it may not be. But we need not doubt that any creature—human or nonhuman—that has such an incentive to investigate the nature of things in their own right will be forever learning more about the practical—life-enhancing—potential of the world he lives in.

That way, of course, lies biological success. Moreover, that way, in the longer run, lie grand science and human civilization too. For it is this love affair with the natural world that drives men and women to their boldest feats of exploration and invention. Richard Dawkins has caught the mood exactly: "After sleeping through a hundred million centuries we have finally opened our eyes on a sumptuous planet, sparkling with colour, bountiful with life. Within decades we must close our eyes again. Isn't it a noble, an enlightened way of spending our

The Enchanted World

time in the sun, to work at understanding the universe and how we have come to wake up in it? This is how I answer when I am asked—as I am surprisingly often—why do I bother to get up in the mornings."[25]

And if Dawkins is not to your taste, let Henri Poincaré say it instead: "The savant does not study nature because it is useful; he studies it because he takes delight in it, and he takes delight in it because it is beautiful. If nature was not beautiful, it would not be worth knowing and life would not be worth living."[26]

8   So That Is Who I Am!

We have been seeking evidence of how, for you as a conscious creature, phenomenal consciousness changes your worldview, so as to change the direction of your life. We have seen first how it makes you care about *pure being* and promotes your *will to live,* and next how it makes you attribute *value and meaning to things* in the external world.

I would say these effects, between them, are quite sufficient to explain why natural selection would have redesigned sensation to give it phenomenal qualities, probably quite early on in evolution, and at any rate long before our ancestors became human.

But the story did not stop there. In the case of human beings—and now I will say humans and their near relatives alone—there turned out to be a payoff on a much grander level: nothing less than the development in each conscious individual of a quite new idea of what it means to be "oneself."

This new—and dramatically inflated—conception of the self arose out of *intellectual reflection* on the effects of consciousness, in part reflection on those very effects outlined earlier.

Intellectual reflection? I mean *puzzling* over these effects, *meditating* on them, *experimenting* with them, *discussing* them with friends—indeed, the very kind of reflection we have been engaged in in this book. Perhaps you will object that this is too much to expect of ordinary people, let alone of our ancestors long ago. I don't believe so. The fact is human beings in general are far too inquisitive, too interested in just who and what they are, to pass over the big questions that consciousness so obviously raises. If humans can be "scientists in the crib," they can be philosophers in the crib—and philosophers for their whole lives too.[1]

◼ Let's step back and begin again with the core self. When you reflect on it, rather than just live it, what strikes you as the most *peculiar* thing about the experience of *being you*?

We have discussed already some of the more remarkable properties of sensations—temporal thickness, and so on. But there is one overarching feature that I expect impresses you before all else, and this is that the experience *is observable by you and no one else.* It is not simply that it *belongs* to you, as, say, your car or your legs belong to you, by virtue of being under your control; it is that it is absolutely *private.* There are no doors between one consciousness and another. Everyone knows directly only of his or her own consciousness and no one else's.

This exceptional aloneness is obvious—even horribly obvious—when you think about it. And you *do* think about it.

I am sure that since childhood you, along with just about everyone else, have played with the riddles that flow from the inaccessibility of other minds. To take John Locke's famous example of seeing colors: how do you know that your color sensation when you see a violet is not like another person's sensation when he or she sees a marigold? The answer, which it has never required a great philosopher to demonstrate, is simply that you do not—because, as Locke said, "one man's mind cannot pass into another man's body."[2] Of course, you long ago ceased to find this conclusion novel. Yet there is no denying how surprising it was at first discovery—and how remarkable it still remains whenever you return to it: not simply an interesting tease but a startling metaphysical revelation.[3]

Indeed, what a strange state of affairs. Nothing else in the world is private in the same way that conscious experience is. Everything else in the world joins up in the four-dimensional space-time manifold that basic physics says is sufficient to describe the universe. But consciousness, it seems, is essentially different. Each individual's consciousness is as much a world apart, on its own plane of existence, as is each separate universe in the "multiverse" that cosmologists sometimes fantasize about. Forget the open doors between one conscious self and another; it seems there is not even the possibility of tunneling through a wormhole.

If you find this situation puzzling—as puzzling as it is wonderful—you are in good company. Your puzzlement is not because you are missing something or cannot think straight (though some professional philosophers persist in saying so). Consciousness, as I had cause to remark in the opening chapter, really is deeply, fascinatingly, and peculiarly private. And

So That Is Who I Am!

the meaning and explanation of this privacy have long posed a major challenge to cognitive science and philosophy of mind.

In part 1 we arrived at our own theory of what lies behind it. According to our model of how sensation arises from monitoring sentition, there will in fact be several reasons why the qualities of your sensations will be accessible to you alone. To start with, you are observing something—the ipsundrum—that you are doing, your own response to stimulation at your body, something that belongs only to you in the same way that any other activity that you initiate belongs only to you. Second, this response has become internalized in the course of evolution, so that what you are observing is, as it happens, literally out of sight of others' eyes. Third, things have been rigged so that you observe your response from a special point of view, the one point from which it appears to have illusory phenomenal properties—so that even if anyone else could observe it, they would not describe it as you do.

It may be true that this does not add up to a *logical lockout,* such as would make your experience unobservable in principle to a third party. As I was at pains to point out in earlier chapters, the Andromedan scientist with super brain-scanning equipment—and a bit of luck—might still discover what it is like for you to have your sensations by reading your brain activity and applying the right theory. Yet, since it is a fact that ordinary human beings have neither the equipment nor the theory, this certainly does add up to a *biological lockout.* And this is quite enough to make the privacy of consciousness hugely impressive, creating the irresistible idea of your self as a separate bubble of consciousness, a separate soul, one self, this self and none other, this secret packet of phenomena. Your body may get as close to another person's body as is physically possible, and yet the bubbles remain essentially inviolate. Share the same body even, like conjoined twins, and there still remain two quite separate consciousnesses.

William James summed up the effective reality: "Absolute insulation, irreducible pluralism, is the law. It seems as if the elementary psychic fact were not thought or this thought or that thought, but my thought, every thought being owned. Neither contemporaneity, nor proximity in space, nor similarity of quality and content are able to fuse thoughts together which are sundered by this barrier of belonging to different personal minds. The breaches between such thoughts are the most absolute breaches in nature."[4]

"Soul," "solo," "isolation." Etymologically, according to the *Oxford English Dictionary,* there is no connection between "soul" as a noun and "sole" as a predicate (though I may say I wonder). But psychologically, the connection is all too clear. No man, so John Donne claimed, is an island entire of himself. Yet surely the truth is that at the deepest level of personal experience, every human being discovers the opposite: when it comes to consciousness, *every man is indeed an island entire of himself.*

But some island! The physicist John Lindner has written: "An ordinary place in the universe is the near vacuum of interstellar space, one atom per cubic meter, three degrees above absolute zero. But you and I are extraordinary places. In us, the universe has become conscious, able to reflect upon itself."[5]

I will come back to this momentous discovery and how it changes your worldview. But let us see where else reflection on consciousness may lead human beings. Next, after private ownership, what would you tell the Andromedan visitor—

So That Is Who I Am!

were she to ask you—about what is so special about being your self? Let us suppose she has picked up on those wonderful questions from the *Ballad for Americans*: "Who are you? What's your racket? What do you do for a living?"[6]

Charles Sherrington had no doubt about what he would say: the primary function of the self—its essential racket—is and has always been to be an *actor* in the world, to *make things happen*. "In the evolution of mind a starting point for 'recognizable' mind lay in its connection with motor acts. Motor behaviour would seem the cradle of recognizable mind. . . . Moreover the motor act is that which seems to clinch the distinction between self and not-self. The doer's doings affirm the self. . . . As far back in the evolutionary tree as intuitions go, amongst them must be that of a subjective 'doing.' . . . The 'I-doing' is my experience of myself in the motor act. It is my mental experience in that phase of my activity. It is, if we prefer, my experience of 'self' explicit in action."[7]

This, we can agree, seems obviously right. Anyone who has observed an infant—human or animal—in the early stages of mastering control over his body will realize how much of the self has, from the beginning, been invested in what Sherrington calls "I-doing." But where does this take you when you ask—of yourself—Sherrington's following question: "This 'I', this self, which can so vividly propose to 'do', what attributes as regards 'doing' does it appear to itself to have?"

Sherrington's answer was simple and unequivocal: "*It counts itself as a 'cause.'*" We can agree again. Certainly it is your "I" that, as the subject of your wishes, is the cause of what you do. But come to think of it, there is something rather remarkable about the role of your "I" in this. The wishes of your

"I" are a *cause* of material events in your body, but as far as you can tell they are not always or even usually an *effect* of material events—in many respects it seems you are a *free* agent, an agent who can generate stuff ex nihilo. Nor is it just motor acts that lie within your power. Thoughts, images, memories, intentions . . . all come when you conjure them.

True, as scientists, we know that this is not the physical reality. Nearly 150 years ago, T. H. Huxley spelled out the true situation:

> Our mental conditions are simply the symbols in consciousness of the changes which take place automatically in the organism. . . . [Thus] the feeling we call volition is not the cause of a voluntary act, but the symbol of that state of the brain which is the immediate cause of that act. We are conscious automata, endowed with free will in the only intelligible sense of that much-abused term—inasmuch as in many respects we are able to do as we like—but none the less parts of the great series of causes and effects which, in unbroken continuity, composes that which is, and has been, and shall be—the sum of existence.[8]

Yet, of course this is not how you yourself see it. For Nature, in designing your mind, has contrived that the chain of causation is largely invisible to you. You as a subject do not have mental access to the events in the brain that *precede* your "deciding to act." The result is that the first you know of your decision is when it is in front of you. And naturally enough, in the absence of evidence to the contrary, you credit your "I" with being the *prime mover* in choosing this action or that.

So That Is Who I Am!

131

No wonder then if you see this as further evidence of the nonphysical status of your conscious mind. As I wrote earlier, everything else in the world joins up in physical space-time—except for phenomenal sensations that are essentially private. Now you find that everything else in the world is the product of preceding material causes—except for your wishes and intentions, which are essentially undetermined.

What do you make of this? What is it like to be an *uncaused cause*? Do you suppose, like Descartes, that you must have a bit of God in you? Do you imagine, as a modern physicist might, that you are your very own big bang? Probably most people's speculations are nothing quite so grand. Yet I do not doubt they are still grand enough to make you reassess your cosmic status. If you have free will, if you can do what you like, *your life is yours.*

■ I said earlier that human beings can be philosophers in the crib. Here is a little girl of twenty-one months, Emily, engaged in what psychologists have actually called "crib talk"—a private monologue just before falling asleep. Emily is thinking about the realpolitik of physical causation.

> The broke, car broke, the . . .
> Emmy can't go in the car.
> Go in green car.
> No.
> Emmy go in the car.
> Broken. Broken.
> Emmy Daddy Mommy go in the car,
> broke,

Da . . . da,
the car . . . their, their, car broken.⁹

At her age she is not so concerned yet with thinking about the causes of what goes on in her own head. But for Christopher Robin, by age six, free-flowing mental causation is at the top of the list.

So—here I am in the dark alone,
There's nobody here to see;
I think to myself,
I play to myself,
And nobody knows what I say to myself;
Here I am in the dark alone,
What is it going to be?
I can think whatever I like to think,
I can play whatever I like to play,
I can laugh whatever I like to laugh,
There's nobody here but me.¹⁰

It is a great thing to discover just how much you, the "I-doer," count for. You move your limbs, you direct your thoughts, you make your plans. You—like a notorious American president—are the "decider." Your doing self is clearly somebody to reckon with.

What is it going to be? What will you create today? What will you bring into the world that was not there before?

Well, how about creating your core self, to start with? Remember that the sensations that give you the feeling of being there arise from your own active response to stimulation of your sense organs. Sensations, from the beginning, involve a sort of doing. This means that, in an important sense, it is your doing self that brings your core self into being. You are responsible at the very deepest level for *what it feels like to be you*. But then, for your next trick, well, how about spreading some of that soul dust onto the things around you? Remember, too, that it is your mind that projects phenomenal qualities onto external objects. If you only knew it, you yourself are responsible for *the feel of the world*.

If you only knew it? But come to think of it—and "come to think of it" is just what human thinkers do—I would say on some level you cannot but *already* know it.

I am not saying you know it up-front. As I wrote in the preceding chapter, "most of the time you never notice your own role in giving things their marvelous qualities—you simply assume that is the way they are made." So, it is true, you often admire things as if, in Proust's words, "it was in them and not in yourself that the divine spark resided."[11] Imagine you are watching a glorious sunrise. You feel lucky to be alive in a world that has so much to offer. You may even be moved, like the poet William Blake, to insist on its supernatural origin. "'What?' it will be Questioned, 'when the Sun rises, do you not see a round Disk of fire somewhat like a Guinea?' O no no. I see an Innumerable company of the Heavenly host crying 'Holy Holy Holy is the Lord God Almighty.'"[12] Such an attitude, as we saw, can and does work wonders for you.

Nevertheless, on some level you must know what the true score is. Thomas Traherne, an earlier English mystic and poet, went straight to the paradoxical heart of it: "By the very right of your senses you enjoy the world. . . . Doth not the glory of the sun pay tribute to *your* sight?"[13] And Traherne's question does not take you by surprise, because just this same thought has already occurred to the philosopher in you. Those red qualia in which that disc of fire is clothed: *who* made them *the way they are*? Already back in the playground you were wondering how the world of colors might look to someone else. And if you could ask yourself then whether the light of the sun you experience as red could be the same light your friend experiences as blue, you are already there. Clearly you did not and do not really believe that phenomenal qualities inhere in things out in the world: at some level, you understand very well your own creative role in it. Oscar Wilde wrote, more than a hundred years ago, "It is in the brain that everything takes place. . . . It is in the brain that the poppy is red, that the apple is odorous, that the skylark sings."[14] Even if you do not actually think of it as happening in your brain, you know it is *you*.

I repeat "at some level" because I expect that you remain genuinely in two minds about this. When nature seems to offer such riches on her own account, you may well be uneasy with the idea she might be borrowing it all from *you*. Indeed, if you felt some alarm on discovering the loneliness of being your core self, how much more difficult it may be to admit the possibility that the universe you are in love with—which may even have seemed to give meaning to your life—is in such a crucial respect your own lonely creation also.

Some years after Wilde, the philosopher Alfred North Whitehead grudgingly acknowledged there might be a scientific case for supposing that "sensations are projected by the mind so as to clothe appropriate bodies in external nature . . .

So That Is Who I Am!

[that] bodies are perceived as with qualities which in reality do not belong to them, qualities which in fact are purely the offspring of the mind." However, he, for his part, was certain this could not be the truth. And his grounds were not so much scientific as *ethical*. For, he said, if it were so, we would have to concede that things in the world *do not have intrinsic value*. And in a famous passage, heavy with sarcasm, he spelled out where that must leave us: "Thus nature gets credit which should in truth be reserved for ourselves: the rose for its scent: the nightingale for his song: and the sun for his radiance. The poets are entirely mistaken. They should address their lyrics to themselves, and should turn them into odes of self-congratulation on the excellency of the human mind. Nature is a dull affair, soundless, scentless, colourless; merely the hurrying of material, endlessly, meaninglessly." And this, Whitehead pronounced, "is quite unbelievable."[15]

However, it would seem Whitehead has seriously underestimated ordinary people's commitment to philosophical inquiry, even when—perhaps especially when—it leads to shocking conclusions. You may not *wish* to believe it all comes from you. But there is no question you *can* believe it. And if and when you realize you have no choice but to believe it, then whatever your initial disappointment, it hits you like a revelation: not of the dullness of nature, but of the *sublimity of your own mind*.

Nor has this escaped the poets. While the nineteenth-century English Romantics, whom Whitehead found so compelling—Wordsworth and Shelley, and the German Romantic Goethe—dwelled on the "haunting presences" out there in nature, German modernism by the 1920s had found a different voice. Rainer Maria Rilke went on to express better than anyone I know the grandeur for *you* of *being here*—and the awful responsibility you thereby bear as the enchanter, the "sayer" of things.

> Why, when this span of life might be fleeted away
> as laurel, a little darker than all
> the surrounding green, with tiny waves on the border
> of every leaf (like the smile of a wind):—oh, why
> *have* to be human, and, shunning Destiny,
> long for Destiny? . . .
>   Not because happiness really
> exists, that precipitate profit of imminent loss.
> Not out of curiosity, not just to practise the heart,
> that could still be there in laurel. . . .
> But because being here is much, and because all this
> that's here, so fleeting, seems to require us and strangely
> concern us. Us the most fleeting of all . . .
> . . . .
>   Are we, perhaps, *here* just for saying: House,
> Bridge, Fountain, Gate, Jug, Fruit tree, Window,—
> possibly: Pillar, Tower? . . . but for saying, remember,
> oh, for such saying as never the things themselves
> hoped so intensely to be.[16]

Being here is much, Rilke tells us, not just on your own account, but because your being here is what is required for all those things around you to become *what you make of them.* Thus it is up to you to project the beam of consciousness out onto the world so that nature can fulfill her promise—so that she can come, as we say, *into her own.*

So That Is Who I Am!

What a job! What a racket! How does it feel, then, for you to be here for that? To be the one who brings it all to life? For it all to be *yours*? Thomas Traherne, for one, could hardly contain himself in his excitement at realizing he was the creator of such splendor: "The streets were mine, the temple was mine, the people were mine, their clothes and gold and silver were mine, as much as their sparkling eyes, fair skins and ruddy faces. The skies were mine, and so were the sun and moon and stars; and all the World was mine, and I the only spectator and enjoyer of it."[17]

Most people are of course more laid back about it. However surprised—alarmed, impressed, proud—you may have been when you first realized the part you yourself are playing in lighting up the world, I assume that by now you have come to take it pretty much for granted. But let's recognize that what you are taking for granted is a kind of miracle, and I have no doubt that behind the scenes it has profoundly shaped your sense of who and what you are. For if you have a miracle at your very center, then *miraculous you are*.

In the two previous chapters we found more than enough positive outcomes of consciousness, at a relatively low level, to keep natural selection interested. But now we are into a different kind of game. It was already something to be a core self. It was something to live in an enchanted world. But now the canopy has been lifted to reveal who is pulling the levers: it is *you*.

If we are looking for ways in which consciousness changes people's psychology, this could be the big one. We have a way to go yet. But let me anticipate where we are heading. Suppose the feeling of transcendent significance that comes from reflecting on consciousness so changes people's sense of their own importance—of what they count for in the wider scheme of things—that it sets a new agenda for human relationships. Then perhaps this opens up a new ecological and cultural niche in which humans can thrive as never before.

But I should not jump the gun on my own argument, or on evolution's. I believe what came first was a new emphasis on the importance of the individual self.

So That Is Who I Am!

9   Being Number One

The "psychological individual" has had a bad press from philosophers and ethicists in recent years. To left and right, there have been scholars ready to declare that individualism is a modern European invention, a product of the Enlightenment or even modern capitalism—never of Nature.

The art historian Jakob Burckhardt famously claimed: "In the Middle Ages . . . Man was conscious of himself only as a member of a race, people, party, family, or corporation—only through some general category. In Italy this veil first melted into air; an *objective* treatment of the State and of all the things of this world became possible. The *subjective* side at the same time asserted itself with corresponding emphasis; man became a spiritual *individual*, and recognized himself as such."[1] In the same vein, the literary critic Peter Abbs, discussing "the historical development of self-consciousness," wrote of "that complex dynamic of change which separated the person from his world making him self-conscious and self-aware, that change in the structure of feeling which during the Renaissance shifted from a sense of unconscious fusion with the world towards a state of conscious individuation."[2]

Among anthropologists, Marylyn Strathern has been influential in arguing that the traditional—and by implication prehistorical—way for human beings to see themselves has been as "dividuals" whose personhood and even whose body is partly shared by the social group.[3] Desmond Tutu, explaining the Swahili concept of Ubuntu, writes, "You cannot be human in isolation. A solitary human being is a contradiction in terms. You are human precisely because of relationships: you are a relational being or you are nothing."[4]

Douglas Hofstadter, extending his ideas about strange loops to human relationships, concludes, "In the end we are all part of one another."[5] And Nietzsche: "Consciousness is really only a net of communication between human beings. . . . My idea is, as you see, that consciousness does not really belong to man's individual existence but rather to his social or herd nature."[6]

It is a strong lineup (to which we could add many more),[7] a lineup, the subtext sometimes reads, *on the side of the best human values*: for who could dare assert the *moral* claim of individualism against dividualism? Nonetheless, I think this attempt to derogate the "individual" misses the essential psychological point. No doubt human beings have always had ways of seeing themselves other than as isolated selves. And the emphasis on the individual or the collective has varied in human groups at different times and places.[8] Yet, even if people *can* think of themselves as parts of the collective, even if sometimes they *should* do so, there is still no way that they cannot also be aware of their essential singularity. For the phenomenology of conscious sensation guarantees that this is where every individual starts—as just that, an individual. What is more, as I will argue shortly, primary individualism, although not uncomplicated, is a highly beneficial trait for the individual in question *and* for the social group as well. If morality comes into it, the moral good arises not through denying individualism but through extrapolating it.

▪ So, I have some explaining to do. I must explain, to start with, what I understand as constituting the larger "personal self"—and then why this self too remains a *phenomenal individual* even as its scope and powers expand.

I quoted Sherrington in the previous chapter on the subject of the self and action. But I also quoted him earlier where, in a famous passage from another book, he wrote more grandly of the self as a unified "psychical existence." The passage continues:

> Each waking day is a stage dominated for good or ill,
> in comedy, farce or tragedy, by a *dramatis persona*, the
> 'self.' And so it will be until the curtain drops. This self
> is a unity. The continuity of its presence in time, some-
> times hardly broken by sleep, its inalienable 'interiority'
> in (sensual) space, its consistency of view-point, the
> privacy of its experience, combine to give it status as a
> unique existence. Although multiple aspects character-
> ize it it has self-cohesion. It regards itself as one, others
> treat it as one. It is addressed as one, by a name to
> which it answers. The Law and the State schedule it as

one. It and they identify it with a body which is considered by it and them to belong to it integrally. In short, unchallenged and unargued conviction assumes it to be one. The logic of grammar endorses this by a pronoun in the singular. All its diversity is merged in oneness.[9]

Clearly this dramatis persona—let us call it now the Ego—is something of a different order from the "core self" that has figured in our discussion of consciousness so far. This larger self is indeed a complex, multifaceted entity: not only a self that feels and does, but one that thinks, perceives, remembers, dreams, desires—a veritable factory, with different specialized divisions, whose product is a whole person with a life story.

Yet, as Sherrington stresses, this Ego is unified. So, what does this amount to at the level of phenomenology? Who or what is at the center of the grand unified self? Whatever it is, it may not be an easy thing to say. You may think I have come up with some unattractive neologisms earlier in this book. So, how about philosopher Galen Strawson's latest: "SESMET"—short for "subject- of-experience-as-single-mental-thing"?[10] But to name it does not resolve its status. The Brazilian author Clarice Lispector, writing at the age of nineteen in her debut stream-of-consciousness novel, *Near to the Wild Heart*, expressed her own puzzlement as well as anyone: "How curious that I'm unable to say who I am. . . . The moment I try to speak, not only do I fail to express what I feel, but what I feel slowly transforms itself into what I am saying."[11]

It may seem we are back with Descartes in his whirlpool. Yet why should we be so scared of taking hold? If you reflect on what is going on when you claim—as no doubt you would—to be *one self*, I am sure your immediate sense of it will be that what makes your Ego a unity is simply the fact that the different components all take your "I" as the subject: "I" feel, "I" think, "I" perceive, "I" remember, "I" dream, "I" desire, and so on, *the same "I" in each case*. And the explanation, if we now unpack this using more technical language, is surely nothing more mysterious than these three points:

First, the mental activities of feeling, thinking, perceiving, willing, and so on, are all "intentional states" in the sense we defined earlier: states that are *about* something (although certainly about different kinds of things).

Second, because they are about something, each of these states must have *a subject* for whom they are about whatever it is—the subject to whom the feelings, thoughts, perceptions, or volitions respectively are being represented.

Third—and here is what is so special—all of these states do, as it transpires, have *one and the same* subject. So all the representations are, as it were, ending up on the same desk (or being displayed on the same instrument panel in the cockpit of your mind), where they can engage in free and easy cross talk.[12]

Now, since you do indeed experience things as being this way in your own case, you may well assume that it could hardly be otherwise. But as theorists, we have to recognize that the unity of the Ego, which you take for granted, is by no means a *logical necessity*. In principle, there is no reason why an individual's brain/mind could not contain several intentional agents operating relatively independently of each other. There could in fact be several disconnected "I"s.

In pathological cases, the unity of the self does sometimes radically break down.[13] And, of course, it can happen in everyday experience that parts of your mind sometimes wander, get lost, and return. When you have come around from a deep sleep, for example, you may even find yourself having to gather your self together bit by bit.

Proust provides a nice description of just this peculiar experience. "When I used to wake up in the middle of the night," he writes, "not knowing where I was, I could not even be sure at first who I was; I had only the most rudimentary sense of existence, such as may lurk and flicker in the depths of an animal's consciousness. . . . But then . . . out of a blurred glimpse of oil-lamps, of shirts with turned-down collars, [I] would gradually piece together the original components of my ego."[14]

Is this how things start out in infancy? Do human babies not have a unified sense of self? Every student of infant behavior would tell us they do not. Indeed, I myself have argued, in an essay that takes off from observations of my two-month-old son, that for the first few months of life the mind of a human baby really must be host to a variety of unallied subselves, separate "I"s.[15] In which case the question becomes: what brings about the unification that will, by the age of three years or so, become the child's normal state. Presumably it is not imposed from outside (although, as Sherrington suggests, other people's expectations may well play an important part). Instead, the infant has somehow to *learn* to be a single Ego. He has—literally—to self-organize the parts of his mind into a single whole.

How is this is done? There are not many answers out there, so I dare mention my own. I believe it is a matter of the components of the mind, which are initially relatively independent, being dynamically linked as *participants in a common enterprise*. Rather in the same the way that the divisions in a factory become part of the same business because they are jointly contributing to manufacturing the final product that will go on sale, rather as members of a band come to be bound together as an artistic unit because they are jointly creating one work of music, so the components of your mind become united as your Ego because they are involved in the common project of creating your singular life: steering *you*—body and soul—through the physical and social world. Within this larger enterprise, each of the subselves may indeed still be doing its own thing: providing you with sensory information, with intelligence, with past knowledge, goals, judgments, initiatives, and so on. But the crucial point is that each subself, in doing its own thing, shares a final path with all the other selves doing their own things. And the evolution of this production system over the first year of life gradually brings the initially separate "I"s into correspondence. In short, your subselves become co-conscious through collaboration.[16]

But now, what qualities accrue to the Ego? How far do you, as this larger self, remain private and singular? Let us note—as we already did in the first chapter—that many of the mental representations of which you are the subject are not as *intrinsically private* as conscious sensations are. Indeed, the content of your thoughts, perceptions, wishes, and other kinds of intentional states that lack phenomenal quality in their own right can, in principle, be relatively easily externalized and shared (most obviously by language, but by nonlinguistic means as well). So the fact is the boundaries of your larger Ego are not so unbreachable in principle as those of the core self. The point was well made by Milan Kundera: "My self does not differ substantially from yours in terms of its thought. Many people, few ideas: we all think more or less the same, and we exchange, borrow, steal thoughts from one another. However, when someone steps on my foot, only I feel the pain. . . . While it suffers, not even a cat can doubt its unique and uninterchangeable self."[17]

Yet—here's the thing—while Kundera is no doubt correct to say that your self "in terms of its thought" does not have the same unique status that your self as a sufferer does, this really is not how it comes across to you. The fact is you do not regard your thinking self as somehow less personal, less special, less *yours*. And the reason for this is that your larger self is unified *under* the core self.

What has happened is that your core self, that "rudimentary sense of existence" around which Proust found the other parts reassembling, has emerged as *first among equals*. And the reason the core self becomes leader of the pack is just that, as we discussed in chapter 6, the phenomenal qualities of sensation, especially the illusion of temporal thickness, give the core self a *substantial existence*. Here, in your mind, is *where the weight is*; this is the self that can take the strain; this provides the continuity. Thoughts, memories, volitions, come and go, but you are always living in the presence of sensations. Thus your core self—the self who *is* because it feels—has become de facto *also* the self who thinks, perceives, remembers, dreams, desires, and ultimately wills the body into action. Every one of your "I"s is now an honorary *phenomenal subject*—by proxy, as it were.

We saw in chapter 7 how "borrowed phenomenality transforms the world into an awesome place." Now, although the explanation is quite different, we might equally say that borrowed phenomenality has transformed your Ego into "an awesome being." In particular, the astonishing singularity of your self as the subject of phenomenal sensations has been extended to your whole Ego. You seem indeed to be an island, not just as a sufferer but as an entire mental self. An *inhabited* island, mind you. Here is where all those bits and pieces of you live: live and enjoy the easy cross talk between themselves, which is so much harder to establish across the borders to another person. If I may push the metaphor, imagine an ocean of islands, each with its own internal world of shared ideas, dreams, desires, and able to communicate to its neighbors only by smoke signals.[18]

But of course you already know all this. I am sure I have described only what is obvious to you: that as a conscious human being you naturally think of yourself as an individual with a separate and unique psychic existence. If there has been a strong tide running in the academic community against this all-too-obvious idea, then as scientists we should resist it. In this book we are discussing consciousness in evolution. We want to know what consciousness *does*. And if we were to let ourselves be swayed by deniers of the self into underestimating what is arguably one of the most significant aspects of how consciousness affects human lives, we would miss the point.

The point is that psychological individualism, when it arose as the inevitable consequence of people's reflecting on what it is like to be a conscious Ego, transformed the landscape in which human beings conducted their affairs. "Egoism"—let us now unashamedly call it that—acquired new levels of justification and found new outlets in people's plans and ambitions, both for themselves and, as we will see, for others.

To start with, the distinction between *me* and *not me* must have assumed an absolute importance it never had before. William James, as always, states the case bluntly and elegantly:

> One great splitting of the whole universe into two halves is made by each of us; and for each of us almost all of the interest attaches to one of the halves; but we all draw the line of division between them in a different place. When I say that we all call the two halves by the same names, and that those names are "*me*" and "*not-me*" respectively, it will at once be seen what I mean. The altogether unique kind of interest which each human mind feels in those parts of creation which it can call *me* or *mine* may be a moral riddle, but it is a fundamental psychological fact. No mind can take the same interest in his neighbor's me as in his own. The neighbor's me falls together with all the rest of things in one foreign mass against which his own me stands out in startling relief.[19]

"Startling relief," James writes. But this is hardly strong enough. It is not just that your conscious Ego shines more brightly than your neighbor's or creates a bigger wave. It is that your Ego *exists* for you as an observable entity in a way that your neighbor's does not. You could not take the same interest in your neighbor's Ego even if you wanted to—simply because you know so much less about it.

But now, what kind of "interest"? Again the word hardly seems strong enough. Elsewhere James writes: "Each of us is animated by a *direct feeling of regard for his own pure principle of individual existence*, whatever that may be." Further on he asks: "What self is loved in 'self-love'?" The term "self-love" is good. But I would say that "self-esteem," coupled with "self-entrancement," might get closer to the reality of the emotion. Remember James's words I quoted earlier: "To have a self that I can *care for*, nature must first present me with some *object* interesting enough to make me instinctively wish to appropriate it for its *own* sake." Now, in presenting you with your conscious Ego, Nature has done just that—with knobs on. For what "interests" you is precisely this awesome *treasure island*.

And you instinctively value this Ego for its own sake? I would say, instinctively, yes, and *rationally* too because your Ego never ceases to amaze and fascinate you. This is to say more than I did in chapter 6, where I expounded the pleasures a conscious creature takes simply in "being there." Now we mean business on a different scale. Not just the pleasures of being there, not even just the pleasures of being there as a somebody, but the pleasures of being there as *who you are and are becoming*.

Oscar Wilde put it in his own narcissistic way: "The aim of life is self-development. To realize one's nature perfectly—that is what each of us is here for."[20] And again: "To love oneself is the beginning of a lifelong romance."[21] But narcissistic or not, Wilde was right on the mark so far as the biological impact of this goes. Once it becomes your purpose to nourish and preserve your conscious Ego, you become a very different kind of operator in the world. Once you anchor your plans and ambitions to the existence of this amazing thing, *me*, you become *naturally* the kind of being that aspires not only to *be your self*, through continually affirming your presence in the world, but to *make more of your self* through learning, creativity, symbolic expression, spiritual growth, social influence, love of others, and so on.

Chapter 9

■ I said "love of others." How so? Let me come to the surprise that, as I have already hinted, human egoism has always had in store. I have been arguing that consciousness separates and isolates people, and so I believe it does; that it promotes individualism, and so I believe it does. But this is by no means the end of the affair.

We know from research in child psychology that human infants acquire a unified sense of self in the first few years of life. The three-year-old has already become an Ego who is fascinated by his own developing story as an individual. Yet what happens next makes up for all the latent and actual narcissism. For no sooner does the child discover the glories of being *me* than he is led to a daring speculation about the selves of other human beings: "If I have this astonishing phenomenon, known only to me, at the center of my existence, then isn't it likely, even certain, that the same holds for other people too?"

I don't say that anyone thinks it through in any such explicit way to reach this aha! revelation. The acquisition by a child of what scientists call a theory of mind, which can be applied to other people, comes slowly through social interaction, exploration, and experiment.[22] It dawns gradually on the child, even hesitantly, that he can attribute phenomenal consciousness to others. But once it comes, his outlook on life, the universe and everything has to undergo a radical adjustment. For he has stumbled upon a truth second only in importance to the truth of being conscious in himself: "It's not just me." Everyone else is a self-sufficient hub of consciousness. All human beings have been endowed by the creator with an inalienable and inviolable mind space of their own, that is just as special, just as private, just as precious and important to them as mine is to me.

Traherne delightedly expressed this side of things: "You never enjoy the world aright, till the Sea itself floweth in your veins, till you are clothed with the heavens, and crowned with the stars: and perceive yourself to be the sole heir of the whole world, and more than so, because men are in it who are every one sole heirs as well as you."[23]

What human beings wake up to is that they are indeed a part of *a society of selves*. The idea is extraordinarily potent—on psychological, ethical, and political levels. And there can be no question that from the moment it took off among our ancestors, it must have been highly adaptive. For from the beginning it would have transformed human relationships, encouraging new levels of mutual respect, and greatly increasing the value individuals placed on their own and others' lives.

I have made much in this chapter of my quarrel with theorists who underestimate human individualism. But as you will see now, my argument about the centrality of the Ego does not so much contradict as set the stage for those who plead the case for "dividualism." I quoted Desmond Tutu above: "You are human precisely because of relationships: you are a relational being or you are nothing." It is a fine sentiment—and one I may now say that it is not only compatible with but actually dependent on the truth of what I have been arguing. Human beings need relationships. But the deepest and best relationships are going to be those between individuals who recognize the existence in others of a conscious self that is as strange and precious—and private—as their own. Every one a *soul* in good standing, the equal of themselves.

PART THREE

10 Entering the Soul Niche

 At a conference on science and spirituality in 2009, the philosopher of physics Michel Bitbol opened his lecture as follows:

Yesterday evening, I wondered how exactly I would connect our topic of this morning [quantum mechanics and the observer] with the broader issue of spirituality that is at the center of this conference. . . . I am not convinced that one can formulate an exhaustive characterization of spirituality, but let me state at least one important aspect and source of it. This source is the continuous, never completely digested astonishment of *being there,* being in this unique situation: why do I live now, in this special period of history? Why am I me, born in this family, in this place of the world? I was taught that there were many other possibilities: being any person, at any time, or even just *not being at all*. And yet here I am, in front of you. Me, not you; here, not there; now, not then. . . . What is the reason, if any, of this inescapable singularity? Does the fact that we all live through this mystery, alleviate it in any way? There is a deep, old, and permanent sense of awe which is associated to such realization of our situation, and I am convinced that this experience is a crucial ground of spirituality as opposed to science. For, how could we take care of the sense of uniqueness and fate that pervades our lives from an undefined moment of our childhood until the unique moment of our own death, if we stick to the methodologically objective discipline of science?[1]

Bitbol does not use the term "soul." But it will not have escaped your notice—and possibly even your censure—that I myself have been using the word with increasing frequency since the beginning of the book. Should I really be using it so freely? Doesn't the word "soul" carry too much baggage? Yes, it does, and I should—I should *because* it does.

At the end of his discussion of "mind-stuff," early in the *Principles of Psychology*, William James wrote: "Many readers have certainly been saying to themselves for the last few pages: 'Why on earth doesn't the poor man say *the Soul* and have done with it?'" He noted that there might be methodological problems with going down that road. Nonetheless, said he, "I confess . . . that to posit a soul influenced in some mysterious way by the brain-states and responding to them by conscious affections of its own, seems to me the line of least logical resistance."[2]

And yet, three chapters later, James was having none of it. Admittedly, he wrote, "The theory of the Soul is the theory of popular philosophy." Admittedly, it would seem to have practical uses—among other things it guarantees the "closed individuality of each personal consciousness" and underpins the idea of "forensic responsibility before God."[3] "The *consequences* of the simplicity and substantiality of the Soul are its incorruptibility and natural *immortality*—nothing but God's direct *fiat* can annihilate it—and its *responsibility* at all times for whatever it may have ever done."

But all this, James claimed, is metaphysics, not science. And "as *psychologists*, we need not be metaphysical at all." In short, "altogether, the Soul is an outbirth of that sort of philosophizing whose great maxim, according to Dr. Hodgson, is: 'Whatever you are *totally* ignorant of, assert to be the explanation of everything else.'" And "My final conclusion, then, about the substantial Soul is that it explains nothing and guarantees nothing. . . . I therefore feel entirely free to discard the word Soul from the rest of this book."

That James had taken 350 pages to get to this point—and had become so tetchy—suggests more than a little internal conflict. You can almost hear a rational soul-denying *ego* battling it out with an emotional soul-affirming *id*. The rationalist wins the argument (that is what rationalists always do). But it is remarkable what hard work it seems to have been—how stubbornly something inside him clung to the big idea.

Well, James was free to do what he liked. It was *his* book. But this is *mine*. And I make no apology for not following James's lead. Even if it is true that as scientific psychologists we need not be metaphysical—no more than our visiting Andromedan scientist need be—we need not and should not be blind to the role of metaphysical ideas in boosting the morale of ordinary human beings. As Bitbol said so eloquently, from childhood until the day you die, you find yourself living at the center of a metaphysical mystery. You cannot but be fascinated by the facts of your own psychical existence. Like it or not, you see yourself, in James's words, as a "simple spiritual substance in which the various psychic faculties, operations, and affections inhere." If that is not to have a soul, I do not know what is.

◼ The theologian Keith Ward has written: "The whole point of talking of the soul is to remind ourselves constantly that we transcend all the conditions of our material existence; that we are always more than the sum of our chemicals, our electrons, our social roles or our genes. . . . We transcend them precisely in being indefinable, always more than can be seen or described, subjects of experience and action, unique and irreplaceable."[4]

So, here is where I am driving. For members of the human species to live in a world where people in general have *this opinion* of themselves—and the opinion is in fact nearly universal— is to live in what we may call the "soul niche." I mean "niche," now, in the conventional ecological use of the term—an environment to which a species has become adapted and where it is designed to flourish. Trout live in rivers, gorillas in forests, bedbugs in beds. Humans live in soul land.

Soul land is a territory of the spirit. It is a place where the magical interiority of human minds makes itself felt on every side. A place where you naturally assume that every other human being lives, as you do, in the extended present of phenomenal consciousness. Where you acknowledge and honor the personhood of others, treating everyone as an independent, respectable, responsible, free-willed conscious being in his or her own right. Where you recognize and celebrate the awesome possibilities of individual, private joy and suffering.

It is a place where the fate of your own consciousness and that of others is a constant talking point. Where souls are the topic of gossip, of tender concern, of mean speculation. Where souls are the subject of prayer and spells and ritual management.

It is a place where the claims of the spirit begin to rank as highly as the claims of the flesh. Where you join hands with others in sharing—sharing, paradoxically, each in yourself—the beauties of the world you have enchanted. Soul land is the natural home of the artists, monks, and popular philosophers (as James would call them) whom I have quoted so liberally throughout this book—a land fit for the heroes of consciousness to live in. I could go on in this vein, but I do not need to. You live there. You know.

Anyone who studies the natural history of human beings must recognize that this spiritual territory is not only where almost all humans do live but where they *give of their best*. There can be no question that this is the niche to which the human species is *biologically* adapted, where individual men and women are able to make the most of their opportunities for leaving descendants. And yet this niche is in many ways a *cultural* product, by no means a given of the natural world. Human beings have largely *invented* the soul niche.

We should not be surprised to find culture giving a leg up to nature in this case. Many other animal species besides humans play an active role in constructing the ecological niche to which they are biologically adapted, by modifying the local physical and social environment.[5] Beavers change the geography by building dams, termites create a whole new eco-climate within their mounds, baboons construct a network of social relationships that helps shelter them from natural hazards and allows them to live in a range of otherwise inhospitable terrains.

Humans, however, have taken "niche construction"—especially social niche construction—to a quite new level. Ian Hacking, the philosopher, has drawn attention to how humans "make up people": they create roles for individuals to adopt, roles that may never have existed before, which then become confirmed as "human kinds," partly because other people encourage the role-players to live up to what is expected of them.[6] In fact, almost all the categories humans use to structure the landscape of their society—such ordinary categories as, say, woman, priest, footballer, clown, Frenchman, beggarman, thief—have been partly created and subsequently reinforced by a looping process of this sort. More to the point, the same is true of extraordinary categories too. Even when a role is, strictly speaking, an impossible or a meaningless one, it can still be one to which individuals are encouraged to aspire and that they may end up simulating. Thus, for example, although it is presumably impossible to be a "witch," many a poor woman in medieval Europe, coming under pressure from the community, embraced this impossibility and did indeed *become a witch of sorts*.

But the most surprising and exotic example of a made-up human kind is the most ordinary of all: namely, the basic category of "human being" as such. Anthropologists have provided rich accounts of how human cultures everywhere believe that human beings—at any rate the members of *their* human tribe—belong to a class of being elevated above the rest of nature. Even if no one can, in reality, live up to the job description of a supra-animal and even a supraphysical being that the culture advertises, people who believe in the possibility for themselves do become *such beings of a sort*.

This is not the place to review such an extensive literature. Instead, to make the point generically, I'll rely on a passage from the essayist Cabell. I have already quoted him in an earlier chapter on the subject of how a human being, who begins with "very little save a faculty for receiving sensations," becomes "a very gullible consciousness provisionally existing among inexplicable mysteries." Cabell is an eccentric and pompous writer. But these words on the subject of how people have gone on to invent themselves, by *living their dreams*, are unexpectedly wise.

> And romance tricks [the human being], but not to his harm. For, be it remembered that man alone of animals plays the ape to his dreams. Romance it is undoubtedly who whispers to every man that life is not a blind and aimless business, not all a hopeless waste and confusion; and that his existence is a pageant (appreciatively observed by divine spectators), and that he is strong and excellent and wise: and to romance he listens, willing and thrice willing to be cheated by the honeyed fiction. The things of which romance assures him are very far from true: yet it is solely by believing himself a creature but little lower than the cherubim that man has by interminable small degrees become, upon the whole, distinctly superior to the chimpanzee: so that, however

extravagant may seem these flattering whispers to-day, they were immeasurably more remote from veracity when men first began to listen to their sugared susurrus, and steadily the discrepancy lessens.[7]

Cabell is surely right that human beings have *talked themselves* into having this grandiose picture of themselves. And the more they have talked themselves up, the taller they have truly grown. Yet, all the while, and for every new individual, it begins with the in-your-face mystery of *being there*.

■ Can we begin to guess how far back in history this goes, when human beings first became denizens of this niche of their own making? I rather doubt it happened "by interminable small degrees"; I think, more likely, there would have been a rush of invention once the ideas first got off the ground. Assuming it depended on language, the tipping point can hardly have predated the emergence of modern humans in Africa 200,000 years ago. But maybe it was much more recent, coinciding with—perhaps indeed being responsible for—the Upper Paleolithic revolution that began in Europe not more than 50,000 years ago.

The question is, are there any kinds of portraits in the archaeological record that would allow us to place the arrival of souls on the scene at least *so far* back in history? I like to think there may be. At any rate, I will share an intriguing observation with you. In the village of Vilafamés, in the Valencia region of Spain, there is a cave just below the castle where there are rock paintings that date to about 15,000 BC. When I visited the cave in 2006, I was taken aback to see the resemblance between one

Figure 12
Rock painting, Vilafamés,
Spain.

Figure 13
Figure from Humphrey,
(2000, p. 249).

of the images (figure 12)[8] and a drawing I made for a scientific journal several years earlier (figure 13).[9] My drawing was intended to illustrate the "privatization of sensation." You will see why the thought immediately occurred to me that the ingoing spiral in the head of the humanoid figure on the left was meant by the Neolithic artist to signify *containment, privacy*—the essential qualities of conscious selfhood.

But if so, let me take the speculation a bit further. What about all those other spirals, cups, and rings within rings—designs that might seem to speak so strongly of *interiority*—that, painted or pecked into the stone, are a recurring theme in rock art from the Neolithic and Bronze ages of human history all over the world, not only in Europe but also across Asia, Australia, and America? Archaeologists have had no good theories of what such symbols are about. It has been suggested that multiple representations, such as that from the Iveragh Peninsula, Ireland (figure 14), are some kind of "field plan." Or perhaps

Entering the Soul Niche

Figure 14.
Rock art panel at Derrynablaha, Iveragh Peninsula, Ireland.
Photograph by Ken Williams, reproduced by permission.

they are merely decorative doodles, without meaning. I would
suggest, with all due reservation, that they are in fact graf-
fiti recording the presence of conscious human beings. Soul
plans, if you like. As I wrote on the opening page of this book:
Here live souls.

11 Dangerous Territory

"Here live souls." But today we must surely say, "Here *lived* souls." For whether I am right about the rock art symbols or not, what is certain is that the human beings who made those marks are *here no longer.* The marks on the rock persist, the individual people do not.

We could take the discussion in a hundred directions from here on. But given the agenda of this book, there is one big problem outstanding: the question of consciousness and death. It is a subject we visited in chapter 6. But we have moved on since then. The original core self has grown into a larger and more estimable entity, the Ego, and now the soul, and presumably people's attitudes to death, will have evolved alongside. I argued earlier that humans, alone among animals, are capable of fearing death. But if oblivion—the absence of sensation—which follows the death of the core self, was already a frightening prospect for human beings, then complete psychic extinction—the absence of memory, personality, knowledge, skills—which follows the death of the soul, has to be more frightening still.

As Susanne Langer has written: "And with the rise and gradual conception of the 'self' as the source of personal autonomy comes, of course, the knowledge of its limit—the ultimate prospect of death. The effect of this intellectual advance is momentous. Each person's deepest emotional concern henceforth shifts to his own life, which he knows cannot be indefinitely preserved."[1]

Potentially this is the major down side of psychological individualism. The higher you climb, the harder you fall. As the future of the individual Ego has acquired ever-greater psychological significance in the course of human evolution, so the death of this Ego must surely have come to be seen as an ever-greater tragedy—a tragedy for that one person who loved himself and a tragedy for the others who loved him too.

The *particular person* has gone, the very person whose consciousness and intellect were designed by Nature to make him believe himself a being of such singular importance. We can hardly underestimate the loss involved. Yevgeny Yevtushenko said it for us:

> No people are uninteresting.
> Their fate is like the chronicle of planets.
> Nothing in them is not particular,
> and planet is dissimilar from planet.
> . . . .
> In any man who dies there dies with him
> his first snow and kiss and fight.
> It goes with him.
> . . . .

Not people die but worlds die in them.
They perish. They cannot be brought back.
The secret worlds are not regenerated.
And every time again and again
I make my lament against destruction.[2]

Such a pity. It hurts us even to think of it. And yet, let's stand back if we can. As scientists, we should surely recognize that for you as a human being to lament the loss of this however-so-interesting individual—even to lament it in advance—may not be such a bad thing, from the point of view of biological survival. We have already remarked in the earlier discussion how your fear of losing the core self will in some circumstances motivate you to go that extra mile to save your own life. Then, by the same token, your fear of losing your larger Ego will presumably provide a stronger incentive still. And just to the extent that you have come to value the Egos of your companions, your soul mates, it will provide an incentive to save their lives too. The more you dread the loss, the more you will actively avoid it. As the evolutionary psychiatrist Randolph Nesse has pointed out in an essay titled "What Good Is Feeling Bad?": "Emotions are set to maximise Darwinian fitness, not happiness."[3]

Thus we might want to argue that the increased death anxiety that has accompanied the rise of individualism has actually been a further way in which consciousness has proved its worth as an adaptation for human beings—another reason for the genes for consciousness to be selected.

■ Maybe there is really some truth in this. But we have only to look more widely at the natural history of consciousness to see that it is clearly not the *whole* truth. In fact, there is more than enough evidence quite to the contrary: the prospect of individual death can sometimes be so deeply depressing as to seriously *damage* biological fitness.

The trouble is that people really *do* die. And although fear of death may sometimes help delay the final reckoning, this is all it can do—*delay* it. It is not the same as, for example, the fear of having your house burn down, which may very well be effective in ensuring that it never happens. With death, in the end, all precautions fail. "Wonders are many on earth, and the greatest of these is man," sings the Chorus in Sophocles' *Antigone*. "There is nothing beyond his power. His subtlety meeteth all chance, all danger conquereth. For every ill he hath found its remedy, save only death."[4]

Human beings can manage with the longest of odds against them, provided there are at least some small grounds for hope. But it is clear that everything changes when you realize your doom is sealed. I have known people (I am among them) who have been knocked back when they first heard of the inevitable heat death of the universe 150 billion years from now. ("What's the point of doing my home-work, then?" was nine-year-old Alvy Singer's response.)[5] The idea that your own soul is not going to survive so much as a paltry one hundred years hardly bears contemplating. Here is W. H. Auden again:

> Lucky the leaf
> Unable to predict the fall. . . .
> But what shall man do, who can whistle tunes by heart,
> Know to the bar when death shall cut him short, like the
>   cry of the shearwater?[6]

Why does it matter so much? The answers may seem obvious, but let's state them anyway. To start with, a hundred years does indeed seem less than a human soul—with its boundless hopes—deserves. To return to Tom Nagel's observations:

> Having been gratuitously introduced to the world by a collection of natural, historical, and social accidents, [a man] finds himself the subject of a *life*, with an indeterminate and not essentially limited future. Viewed in this way, death, no matter how inevitable, is an abrupt cancellation of indefinitely extensive possible goods.... If the normal lifespan were a thousand years, death at 80 would be a tragedy. As things are, it may be just a more widespread tragedy. If there is no limit to the amount of life it would be good to have, then it may be that a bad end is in store for us all.[7]

So, you would *like* to have more. But surely this is not the chief reason why you do not want to die. While the prospect of not getting all those possible goods may make you feel hard done by, it will not in itself make you depressed. Life can still be beautiful even if it is imperfect. No, the bigger problem is that the prospect of death threatens to take away the beauty of life even as you live it—*because it strips life of meaning.* Albert Camus stated it bluntly: "There is but one truly serious philosophical problem and that is suicide. Judging whether life is or is not worth living amounts to answering the fundamental question of philosophy.... Beginning to think is beginning to be undermined."[8]

I would say it comes down to this. Whether life is worth living has become an increasingly serious problem for human beings because of a quite special feature of the way the human mind works: the importance of—and the need for—a *justifying narrative*. As a human, because you have evolved to think of yourself as a responsible individual, you count on having *reasons* for every project you undertake. That is, you, as an Ego, expect to be able to answer the question "*Why* am I doing this?": "Why *must* I...," "Why *ought* I...," "Why *wish* I...to achieve *this* goal by *these* means?" It may be true that, so long as the going is easy and no one challenges you, you will generally let the reasons go unstated. But just so soon as you come up against obstacles or have to make hard choices, then it is your habit to use reasons as *mental drivers*: to motivate you, to direct or redirect your actions, to keep yourself on target.

The development of this kind of rational self-control has, in the course of evolution, brought a new level of intelligence to human endeavors, and also a new level of commitment. You as an Ego *think ahead* to find good *personal reasons* for *acting now*. In so doing you throw a hook to the future by means of which you are able to pull yourself upward.

This special reliance on reasons allows you to be—as no nonhuman animal can be—confident in the rightness, the worthwhileness, of your cause. Typically you *believe* in what you are doing. However, there is a potential danger in this. For the dreadful truth is that your reliance on reasons also allows you to be—as no animal can be—beset by doubts. Indeed, just as the existence of reasons strengthens your resolve, the lack of reasons can and should weaken it. And when you do not believe in what you are doing you may—often you ought to—stop doing it at all. It has been well said that if something is not worth doing, it is not worth doing well. What, then, if you start asking whether life as such is worth the doing?

There will be several obvious short-term answers to be found. But having a life is not a short-term project. Everyone can be famous for fifteen minutes, and no doubt everyone can find happiness and fulfillment for an hour, a day, even a year. But when you ask whether life—your particular life—is *worth living,* you are looking much farther down the road, to the account you might later give of why the sum of what you have experienced and done has been worthwhile.

The trouble is precisely that "beginning to think is beginning to be undermined." Once you start thinking it through, it can become distressingly clear that the reasons you might immediately fasten on to for having a life may not stand critical scrutiny. The philosopher George Santayana said it plainly: the idea "that life is worth living is the most necessary of assumptions and, were it not assumed, the most impossible of conclusions."[9]

How so? What would block you from concluding rationally that life is worth the candle? What is the problem? There is one overriding one: the fact of *death.* For it is death that threatens to undermine just about every good reason you might otherwise come up with for determining that life is—or, at the end of the day, will have been—worth living.

This is not to say that everything would necessarily be fine if you were not going to die. But it is to say that maybe nothing is fine if you are going to die. You throw a hook to the future, and, when you put the weight of your life's purpose on it, *the ground gives way.*

Here is David Hume's summation of the problem: "When we reflect on the shortness and uncertainty of life, how despicable seem all our pursuits of happiness? And even, if we would extend our concern beyond our own life, how frivolous appear our most enlarged and generous projects . . . hurried away by time, lost in the immense ocean of matter?"[10] And here is Woody Allen's: "The experience is just so hopeless and awful and fraught with tragedy. . . . By the end—what is it, after all? It's kind of a meaningless experience that ends with decay and death. It's nothing. . . . It is of no consequence. You live, you die, you're forgotten."[11]

The literary critic George Steiner writes of "the scandal, the incomprehensibility of individual death."[12] "The future tense, the ability to discuss possible events on the day after one's funeral or in stellar space a million years hence, looks to be specific to *homo sapiens*. . . . There is an actual sense in which every human use of the future tense of the verb 'to be' is a negation, however limited, of mortality."

Now, we might think that concerns such as these about the "lack of future" must be a peculiarly modern phenomenon, which can hardly be relevant to the long march of mankind through evolution. The psychoanalyst Carl Jung was of the opinion that even among contemporary humans, "fortunately, in her kindness and patience, Nature has never put the fatal question as to the meaning of their lives into the mouths of most people. And where no one asks, no one need answer."[13] But let us have no hesitation in contradicting him. Knowing what we do of human genius and imagination, we can be quite sure that—Nature's supposed "kindness" notwithstanding—it is simply not true that most people have been created to be too incurious to ask the obvious question or too dull spirited to know a scandal when they see one.

We may not be used to thinking of our ancestors of the Paleolithic era as Hamlets or young Werthers, wandering across the sand—or ice—pondering the pointlessness of existence. But human beings have had brains that are anatomically very much like those we have today for about the last 150,000 years. And charity—but science as well—demands that we should assume they have had minds vulnerable to forms of existential anxiety at least that long.

> O the mind, mind has mountains; cliffs of fall
> Frightful, sheer, no-man-fathomed.[14]

Thus Gerard Manley Hopkins describes, even in the shape of his verse, the vertiginous landscape that people have created for themselves and made their home.

▪ The soul niche, let it be said, *is dangerous territory*. Can a life that is bound to end so pointlessly have had any point to it along the way? Homework is the least of it; why not kill yourself right now? For, of course, you, as a human, if you should want to avoid the pointless future, *always can*. As Erwin Stengel noted: "At some stage of evolution man must have discovered that he can kill not only animals and fellow-men but also himself. It can be assumed that life has never since been the same to him."[15]

True, if you really fear death, you will presumably not kill yourself because of *that*. But if, as may be more the case, you find the prospect of death demoralizing and dispiriting, then suicide could be a rational way out. Why *not*? Why not, with Hamlet, "take arms against a sea of troubles and by opposing end them"? Why not, with Eve in Milton's poem, seek for yourself and off-spring "some relief of our extremes"? "Miserable it is," Eve says to Adam, "to be to others cause of misery.... Childless thou art, childless remain."

Why stand we longer shivering under fears
That show no end but death; and have the power,
Of many ways to die, the shortest choosing,
Destruction with destruction to destroy?[16]

It is not even as if the decision to let go would require unusual courage or commitment, nor be technically difficult. To
end yourself, you have only to omit to preserve yourself. To escape the future, you have only to omit to invest in it. Every time
you walk down a cliff path, every time you take the wheel of a
car, every time you swim beyond your depth, the smallest of actions—or inactions—would do the job.

"How thin the line between the will to live and the will
to die," Susan Sontag suggests. "How about a hole . . . a really
deep hole, which you put in a public place, for general use. In
Manhattan, say, at the corner of Seventieth and Fifth. . . . A sign
beside the hole reads: 4 PM–8 PM / MON WED & FRI / SUICIDE
PERMITTED. Just that. A sign. Why, surely people would jump
who had hardly thought of it before."[17]

In 1913 Ludwig Wittgenstein told a friend that "all his life
there had hardly been a day, in which he had not thought suicide a possibility."[18] More typically, among today's American
high school students, 60 percent say they have considered kill-
ing themselves, 14 percent have thought about it seriously in the
last year, and 5 percent have attempted it—more than one million students a year.[19]

If—it is, of course, a big "if"—such has been the pattern
since human beings first started to ask whether life is worth living, it means there must have been a severe challenge for our
ancestors to discover defensive measures, whether at the level of
culture or biology. For there is no question that any tendency

to suicide—or childlessness, which comes to the same thing—could not but pose a serious threat to the continuity of the human species. In fact, if unchecked, it would certainly have been terminal.

How many direct parental ancestors have you had in the last fifty thousand years? With an intergeneration time of twenty-five years and two parents per generation, the answer must be many millions.[20] But we know for a fact that among all the individuals in the lines that led to you there cannot have been a single one who, worrying about the ultimate pointlessness of life, chose early on to end it or to forsake his or her infant offspring. Indeed, if there had been so much as a thousandth of a chance of any one of those millions doing so, the probability of your being here now would be near zero.

Yet while none of them *did* it, it seems only too likely that many, even most of them, *did think* of it. And let's note, by the way, that suicidal thoughts need not be chronic, everyday thoughts to be lethal. Being tempted to kill yourself just once a year—in the course of an otherwise happy life—could still spell termination. For living and dying have different tenses: the first requires continuing imperfect investment, the second only a perfect single act. "I have set before you life and death, blessing and cursing, therefore choose life that thou and thy seed may live," says the Preacher.[21] But the choice is not symmetrical. Choose the first, and you can still choose the second later; but choose the second, and that's it.

What stops those who *think* from *acting*? Maybe in some cases not enough. Evolution has taken wrong turns before with other species, which have resulted in extinction. Maybe for some branches of the human line this was true also. We know from the evidence of "bottlenecks" in the genetic record—

times when the number of human genes in circulation had been severely reduced—that after the emergence of modern humans, there were several sudden collapses in the human population, which are as yet unexplained.[22] The cause could have been epidemic disease, internecine warfare, or volcanic eruptions. But I wonder: could the cause have been consciousness itself—a conscious self that had become so precious as to be a burden? Søren Kierkegaard writes: "Having a self, being a self, is the greatest, the infinite, concession that has been made to man, but also eternity's claim on him."[23] Did whole groups of humans yield to this claim—lose heart and succumb?

There is no way of knowing the answer. Loss of heart will have left no identifiable trace in the paleoanthropological record. However, we do know for certain that even if those others succumbed, *your* ancestors did not. What was different? What helped your ancestors to make it through? If there is indeed something that stops those who think from acting, it must surely be that *other thoughts* come to mind.

12 Cheating Death

"It takes so little, so infinitely little, for a person to cross the border beyond which everything loses meaning: love, convictions, faith, history. Human life—and herein lies its secret—takes place in the immediate proximity of that border, even in direct contact with it; it is not miles away, but a fraction of an inch."[1]

So Milan Kundera has written. His message—which is the message of the previous chapter—is that human beings' solution to their existential dilemma has been and is a close call. Kundera labels whatever this solution is a "secret." Yet, as we have stressed all along, *secrets* do not play well with natural selection—or, for that matter, with cultural selection. If human survival has depended on it, this secret must be out in the open, evident in the natural history of consciousness. Our question then should be: looking again at that natural history, what can we see people *doing* and *saying* to fend off despair, to inoculate themselves against the immanent loss of heart?

To answer this question properly would, of course, require telling the whole story of human civilization from the beginning. You will see, however, that this is the next-to-last chapter of the book. What I am about to say must therefore be quite inadequate. But this is a book about the history of consciousness, and I want to round it off by arguing that consciousness had one more trick up its sleeve.

"What shall man do, who knows to the bar when death shall cut him short?" I will review—or at any rate visit—three strategies of restoring meaning to life that are widely on display as human responses to anxiety about death.

- *Discount the future*—and live for the present.
- *Disindividuate*—and identify yourself with cultural entities that will survive you.
- *Deny the finality of bodily death*—and believe the individual self to be immortal.

Discounting the Future

I have remarked often enough in earlier pages that for a phenomenally conscious creature, simply *being there* is a cause for celebration. So, perhaps Walter Hagen had it right:

You're only here for a short visit.
Don't hurry, don't worry.
And be sure to smell the flowers along the way.[2]

When you can, as we have seen, revel in living in the thick moment of the finite present, do you really have to spoil it by worrying about *infinity*? Blaise Pascal, gloomy saint that he was, spoke for the worriers: "When I consider the brief span of my life, absorbed into the eternity before and after—*as the remembrance of a guest that tarrieth but a day*—the small space I occupy and which I see swallowed up in the infinite immensity of spaces of which I know nothing and which know nothing of me, I take fright. . . . The eternal silence of those infinite spaces terrifies me."[3] But the mathematical philosopher Frank Ramsey took a lighter view of things: "I don't feel in the least humble before the vastness of the heavens. The stars may be large, but they cannot think or love; and these are qualities which impress me far more than size does. I take no credit for weighing nearly seventeen stone. My picture of the world is drawn in perspective, and not like a model to scale. The foreground is occupied by human beings, and the stars are as small as threepenny bits."[4]

David Hume, while recognizing, as we saw, that there is indeed an intellectual problem with the prospect of loss of future, boldly announced that it was not in human nature to dwell on it.

> Most fortunately it happens, that since reason is incapable of dispelling these clouds, nature herself suffices to that purpose, and cures me of this philosophical melancholy and delirium, either by relaxing this bent of mind, or by some avocation, and lively impression by my senses, which obliterate all these chimeras. I dine, I play a game of backgammon, I converse, and am merry

with my friends; and when after three or four hours'
amusement, I would return to these speculations, they
appear so cold, and strain'd, and ridiculous, that I cannot find it in my heart to enter into them any farther.[5]

For philosopher Michel Ferrari: "The eternal present of
my 'pure' experience, when I attend to it, is more alive to me
than some later eternity."[6] And for Camus: "If there is a sin
against life, it consists perhaps not so much in despairing of
life as in hoping for another life and in eluding the implacable
grandeur of this life."[7] Meanwhile, Pascal himself reflected:
"We never keep to the present. We anticipate the future as if
we found it too slow in coming and were trying to hurry it up,
or we recall the past as if to stay its too rapid flight. We are so
unwise that we wander about in times that do not belong to
us, and do not think of the only one that does."[8]

Brave talk from the philosophers. But how effective a
strategy is this? Do ordinary people really manage to calm
their fears by living in the present? I think the answer must
be they do and they don't. That is, they do cherish the present,
sometimes as a deliberate defiance of death, but they do not
make their parting with life any the easier by doing so.

The evidence is all around that people will attempt to
pack in as much experience as they can before they go, precisely so as to cheat death of its victory. And the kind of experience they look for in these circumstances does seem to
be overwhelmingly sensory, rather than, say, intellectual or
cultural. In 2003, BBC television asked its viewers what they
would like to do before they die.[9] Twenty thousand people
responded, and in the top fifty things they mentioned, almost

every one of them involved as-yet-untried forms of sensation. The top experiences were classified on a related Web site under four headings: "Earth," "Fire," "Water," "Wind."[10] No one followed Bertrand Russell in saying the one thing they wanted was to know more mathematics.[11]

But let's get particular. This news item appeared in 2001:

> A terminally ill boy had his dying wish granted in Australia this month.... The wish was not for a trip to Disneyland or to meet a famous sports star. Instead, the 15-year-old wanted to lose his virginity before he died of cancer. The boy, who remains anonymous but was called Jack by the Australian media, did not want his parents to know about his request. Because of his many years spent in hospital, he had no girlfriend or female friends. Jack died last week, but not before having his last wish granted. Without the knowledge of his parents or hospital staff, friends arranged an encounter with a prostitute outside of hospital premises.[12]

It makes sense that Jack and others should focus on having *novel* experiences before they die. For there is certainly something different and special about the first time. Yet the record shows that when people are actually facing death in the near future, they are as likely to seek intense experiences as novel ones. Hume observed: "We are informed by Thucydides, that, during the famous plague of Athens, when death seemed present to every one, a dissolute mirth and gaiety prevailed among the people, who exhorted one another to make the most of life as long as it endured. The same observation is made by

Boccac[cio], with regard to the plague of Florence. A like principle makes soldiers, during war, be more addicted to riot and expense, than any other race of men."[13]

It is true that not everyone behaves in this way. Still, if you question how general this phenomenon is, then consider the undoubted evidence relating to the ritual of the last breakfast before execution in the contemporary United States. I have quoted several well-crafted lists of sensory pleasures offered by poets, from Brooke to Hopkins. But here is a rather more surprising list—a prose poem of sorts written by several hands—that could, until recently, be found posted on the Texas Department of Criminal Justice's Web site:

Fried fish fillet, french fries, orange juice, German chocolate cake.

Double meat cheeseburger (with jalapenos and trimmings on the side), vanilla malt, French fries, onion rings, ketchup, hot picante sauce, vanilla ice cream, two Cokes, two Dr. Peppers, and a chicken fried steak sandwich with cheese pickles, lettuce, tomatoes, and salad dressing.

Eight soft fried eggs (wants yellow runny), big bowl of grits, five biscuits with bowl of butter, five pieces of fried hard and crisp bacon, two sausage patties, pitcher of chocolate milk, two pints vanilla Blue Bell ice cream, and two bananas.

One cup of hot tea (from tea bags) and six chocolate chip cookies.[14]

Remarkably, 238 of 301 prisoners executed in Texas between 1982 and 2003 not only chose to give over some of their remaining minutes to eating this last meal, but evidently gave considerable thought to the menu. A menu, mind you, full of familiar things. I find it telling that no one in this situation chose to have a virginal experience with oysters. In 1994 Robert Alton Harris put in his order for "two pizzas, twenty-one pieces of extra-crispy Kentucky Fried Chicken, jelly beans, and a six-pack of Pepsi." Then, the prison officer reports, "He stood in the deathwatch cell and ate this stuff in 'big bites, big bites.'" A few hours later he was killed by poison gas.[15]

Think *consciousness*—think Nature's most astonishing creation—as you read those lists. What is going on? No doubt intense sensation can at least act as a distraction from thoughts about the oblivion that is about to overtake you. While you are living in the present, you are certainly alive. Like the man who is falling from a skyscraper, you can shout to someone at the window as you pass the fortieth floor, "All right so far!" You may even persuade yourself that this present moment is so full of glory that afterward nothing else matters.

Yet, I regret to say, as a rule this is not how human psychology works. Rather, the greater the pleasure experienced, the greater the appetite for more. Would Harris, while savoring the sweet sensation of the jelly beans, have become any better reconciled to his imminent extinction, or would he have wished ever more fervently to be spared so as to have such sensations again? Would Hume as he dined and made merry with his friends have really banished those chimeras permanently, or, at four in the morning, would they have returned with still-greater force? Samuel Johnson was of the opinion that Hume's serenity—which he continued to display even in the days of his final illness—was only a pose, "an appearance of ease" to confound believers.[16] Hume claimed that nature herself turned his thoughts away from death, but I am inclined to side with Pascal when he observed that for a man in a dungeon, waiting to know whether he was to die in an hour, "it would be *unnatural* for him to spend that hour . . . playing piquet."[17]

And then young Jack? I wonder whether it would have been better for him if his sexual encounter had left him disappointed. For it would surely have been easier for him to leave this world if he did not think life—and sex—were such a big deal, easier than if a single experience had made him all the more keenly aware of what he would be missing. Remember Nagel's summary comment that "death . . . is an abrupt cancellation of indefinitely extensive possible goods."

I do not want to seem to preach. The issues are complex and personal. Mary Oliver, in a poem full of courage, "When Death Comes," has written that at the end of her life she wants to be able to say that all along she was "a bride married to amazement . . . the bridegroom, taking the world into my arms."[18]

Perhaps, when it is over, these will truly be Oliver's parting thoughts. But I come back to Rupert Brooke. As we saw, he also declared himself to be in love with the universe—and to be loved in return:

> I have been so great a lover: filled my days
> So proudly with the splendour of Love's praise,
> The pain, the calm, and the astonishment.

Still, he ended his hymn to sensation on a more disillusioned, even angry, note.

Chapter 12
184

All these have been my loves. And these shall pass.
Whatever passes not, in the great hour,
Nor all my passion, all my prayers, have power
To hold them with me through the gate of Death.
They'll play deserter, turn with the traitor breath,
Break the high bond we made, and sell Love's trust
And sacramented covenant to the dust.[19]

"Deserter," "traitor." Brooke will not be reconciled. He returns us to the shocking reality of nature's double-dealing over consciousness: that while she has designed the human soul to look forward to an everlasting marriage to experience, she has at the same time allowed the body that sustains it to seek an early divorce.

The BBC's book has a peculiar title: *Unforgettable Things to Do before You Die.*[20] The trouble is you will *forget everything* when you die.

Disindividuation

Then, where else might you, as an individual, turn for comfort? Perhaps there is a straightforward answer, which is to persuade yourself that, even if you cannot always be there, your *world*, the world *you have made* and *helped propel into the future,* will continue after you are gone.

The first steps at least are easy. It is true that you will forget everything when you die, but not, of course, that *all will be forgotten.* It is true too that you will no longer play a role in lighting up the world, but not that *the world will no longer be lit up.* John Donne, in a terrifying line, asked: "What if this present were the world's last night?"[21] Imagine if your consciousness were the only consciousness there is, so that your death would bring an end to phenomenal properties across the universe. This would certainly be the nightmare case of individual responsibility. And, if you were to believe in it, I am sure you would justifiably succumb to total panic. But why should you even consider it? You live in the soul niche. However special and alone you feel subjectively, you can rest assured it is not just you. Thankfully, Nature has spread the joy.

I have taken a strong line in the earlier chapters in arguing that the individual self, with its bounded consciousness, has to be central to human beings' picture of who and what they are. I do not want to retreat from this position. However, I can see that there is room to move beyond this: there could be additional ways—and perhaps more comforting ways—of seeing things. Dividualism could make some kind of sense after all.

The unified self, I argued earlier, is a construction. During your development as an infant, the components of your individual Ego came to be united as one self because and insofar as they found themselves participating in a common project— the project of creating your life. But suppose, now, this project could be broadened to include not just your first-person's life but the lives of others too. In that case perhaps your self could come to have this wider remit by the very process that it became unified to start with.

Bertrand Russell, as he entered old age, wrote:

> The best way to overcome [the fear of death]—so at least it seems to me—is to make your interests gradually wider and more impersonal, until bit by bit the walls of the ego recede, and your life becomes increas-

ingly merged in the universal life. An individual human existence should be like a river—small at first, narrowly contained within its banks, and rushing passionately past boulders and over waterfalls. Gradually the river grows wider, the banks recede, the waters flow more quietly, and in the end, without any visible break, they become merged in the sea, and painlessly lose their individual being. The man who, in old age, can see his life in this way, will not suffer from the fear of death, since the things he cares for will continue.[22]

I will agree, this sounds good. It sounds quite *natural* too. A relatively selfless interest in the success of your own biological descendants, even after you are dead, must surely have an instinctive basis in the human mind (and of many nonhuman animals too). Thus the evolved sentiments that are apposite to caring for a biological family might be easily extended to the symbolic family or the clan. This would not perhaps amount to "universal life," as Russell puts it, but it could well embrace the life of your culturally defined social group.

Such disindividuation ought indeed to help allay your fears. However, it is not going to leave you free of anxiety about the future. For you still have to worry that "the things you care for" will in fact continue. The buck will have been passed to cultural institutions. And those institutions, although certainly less vulnerable than you are as an individual, are by no means guaranteed to last forever. Cultures can be overthrown by alien forces or decay of their own accord. The history of the world's civilizations is one of unexpected collapses: of empires and Reichs and religions that thought themselves eternal, being wiped off the map. If you are to die happy in the knowledge that the things you personally care for will continue, you have to believe that *your* culture is different.

Recognizing this, Peter Berger and Thomas Luckmann have spelled out the importance of *symbolic* immortality:

> Death posits the most terrifying threat to the taken-for-granted realities of everyday life. The integration of death within the paramount reality of social existence is . . . consequently, one of the most important fruits of symbolic universes. . . . All legitimations of death must carry out the same essential task—they must enable the individual to go on living in society after the death of significant others and to anticipate his own death with . . . terror sufficiently mitigated so as not to paralyse the continued performance of the routines of everyday life. . . . On the level of meaning, the institutional order represents a shield against terror. . . . The symbolic universe shelters the individual from ultimate terror by bestowing ultimate legitimation upon the protective structures of the institutional order.[23]

So, let us ask, do people actually think this way? If they do—if they cope with the threat of personal extinction by identifying with institutions and symbols that will survive them—then we might expect to find them responding to reminders of *individual* death by rushing to defend *cultural* values.

Just such evidence has come from a remarkable body of new research on what happens when human subjects are made to think about mortality. The research has been spearheaded by those involved with so-called terror management theory.[24]

What they have shown, in study after study, is that when people go through what they refer to as a "mortality salience induction"—as, for example, when people spend a few minutes writing about their own deaths, watch a film of a fatal car crash, or simply have the word "dead" flashed on a screen—a number of strong changes in attitude follow. The immediate reaction, predictably enough, tends to be one of defense and denial: the experimental subjects look for reasons why they as individuals are at no immediate risk. But the delayed reaction that emerges once these subjects relax their guard and let subconscious thoughts come through is much more surprising and interesting. In a variety of ways they become more socially conformist and centered on group values, more authoritarian, less understanding or forgiving of deviance, and all the more willing to punish eccentrics and outsiders and to reward mainstream heroes.

Let me cite just a few of the experimental findings. When municipal court judges in the United States were asked to set bail for an alleged prostitute, those who had filled out a questionnaire relating to their own death set the mean bail at $455, whereas those who been questioned about a more neutral topic set it at just $50. When American students were asked to say what they thought about an essay, supposedly written by a foreigner, that either praised the United States or criticized it, those who had been through the mortality salience induction showed an increased liking for the pro-American essayist and a dislike for the anti-American—and when given the opportunity to administer spiteful punishment to the anti-American, were all the more ready to do so. When students were put in a position where, to solve a practical task, they had to sift black dye through an American flag or to hammer in a nail with a crucifix, those who had been through the mortality salience induction showed much greater resistance to carrying out the culturally offensive actions.

Nor are these effects limited to the somewhat contrived situation of the social-psychology laboratory or to Americans. In a study in Germany (subsequently replicated in the United States), mortality salience was manipulated in a more naturalistic setting by stopping people in the street either directly in front of a funeral parlor or a hundred yards before or after it. When subjects were asked to estimate what proportion of the population shared their own view on a controversial political or religious issue, those stopped in front of the funeral parlor showed a marked tendency to overestimate how many other people agreed with them (especially if their opinion was in fact the minority one). In the U.S. study, subjects were asked whether Christian values should be taught in public schools; those who held this view, when questioned in front of the funeral parlor, reckoned that 61 percent would agree with them, but this estimate fell to 42 percent or 46 percent when they were a hundred yards either side.

More than ninety studies in five countries during the 1990s demonstrated the reality of these effects. Then, tragically, in 2001 came real-world confirmation of this research, such as no one could have wished for. After the attack on the World Trade Center on September 11, all the patterns that had been observed to occur after experimentally induced mortality salience emerged with a vengeance across certain sections of the population of the U.S.A. (and to some extent elsewhere): patriotism, flag-waving, exaggerated confidence in national values, derogation of foreigners, antihomosexual sentiments, abuse of prisoners, and so on. The remarks of the fundamentalist Christian preacher Jerry Falwell, on a radio chat show with Pat Robertson a few days after the event, apparently showed the process in full flood: "I really believe that the pagans, and the abortionists, and the feminists, and the gays and the lesbians who are actively trying to make that an alternative lifestyle, the ACLU, People for the American Way—all of them who have tried to secularize America—I point the finger in their face and say, 'You helped this happen.'"[25]

What should we make of these results? The experimental facts are clear and undisputed (so much so, that I would be pretty sure that, with the emphasis on death in what you have just been reading, you yourself will have shifted politically in the last hour).

Though there have been competing interpretations, I think the researchers have made a strong case that people do indeed respond to reminders of mortality by seeking reassurance that their cultural world is stable, lawful, protected from alien influences, and thus potentially eternal.[26] However, it is one thing to provide evidence that this is what people are doing, and another to show that the strategy actually succeeds—succeeds, that is, in what is supposed to be its chief purpose, which is to enable people to overcome the terror of death. For sure, disindividuation, identification with cultural entities that will outlive you, can help relieve some of the pain. Symbolic immortality is of course worth having; it is better than nothing. If you did not have it, you would be in even greater trouble. But can you honestly say that symbolic survival is all—or even a truly significant part—of what you want?

As the Roman poet Horace wrote, "You can drive out nature with a pitchfork, but she will always return." We might equally say you can tame individualism with culture, but it will always fight back. And as you lie awake wondering what will become of you, I doubt you will be able to hide for long behind the conceit that "in the end we are all part of one another." True, there are forms of brainwashing, such as advanced Buddhist exercises (I mean brainwashing in the best sense), that can help to counter individualism. But let no one suggest the end result is achieved without great intellectual effort.

David Galin, a psychiatrist with a special interest in Buddhism, has explained:

> The Buddhist tradition holds that Ordinary Man's inborn erroneous view of self as an enduring entity is the cause of his suffering because he tries to hold on to that which is in constant flux and has no existence outside of shifting contexts. Therefore a new corrective experience of self is needed. Buddhism takes great interest in how people experience their self, rather than just their abstract concept of it, because Buddhist practices are designed to lead to a new (correct) experience. It takes arduous training to modify or overcome the natural state of experiencing the self as persisting and unchanging.[27]

But the "natural state of experiencing the self" is of course the *natural* one. Maybe there are some people who, with or even without arduous training in "correcting" their experience, come to take an interest in the fate of "life in general" or even "mind in general." Yet it is, as a matter of fact, a rare person whose primary concern does not remain his or her own life—the one life "I am living now."

The point was made forcefully by George Howison, a critic of William James, after James had speculated, in a lecture titled "Human Immortality," that after bodily death all separate minds might become folded into some kind of transcendental group mind (the "mother-sea"). Howison retorted: "One weak point in your exposition, as it appears to me, is your failure to connect your argument *securely* with the possibility of *individual* immortality. . . . [If] these transcendental minds are not *ours*, of what earthly avail is their survival of the death of the brain to us?"[28]

Woody Allen said it just as well: "I don't want to achieve immortality through my work; I want to achieve immortality through not dying. I don't want to live on in the hearts of my countrymen; I want to live on in my apartment."[29]

Denying Death

So where next? If human beings cannot bear to be *mortal individuals* with a temporary presence in their physical bodies or to be *immortal dividuals* with a lasting presence in the collective culture, perhaps there is only one way left. They must become *immortal individuals* with a lasting presence in some kind of eternal spirit world.

I said at the end of the previous chapter that bad thoughts can be beaten only by other better thoughts. Since the bad thoughts stem directly from the expectation that your individual consciousness will die when your body dies, then, of course, the best thought of all would be that you need not actually expect this. True, Woody Allen is asking too much when he asks not to die at all. Yet his request points the way to another solution: the continuation of Woody Allen's personal self in a disembodied form. Carl Stumpf, one of the founders of scientific psychology, wrote, in another letter to James, "Personal immortality stands for me in the foreground. . . . The realization of ideals is only possible on the presupposition of individual immortality. Psychical values cannot be added together. This is for me the first condition, if life is not to be absolutely without consolation and meaning."[30]

Of course the one snag is that for this solution to work, you have to *believe* in it. And this may seem rather a tall order. For how could you possibly believe in personal immortality if and when the idea runs completely counter to common sense? Yet, when it comes to it, it may not, after all, be so difficult. And the reason is that your evolved conscious Ego already has everything it takes to drive your thoughts this way. Indeed, far from running counter to common sense, for most human beings belief in personality immortality arguably *is* common sense. Even better, common sense *based on the evidence*.

What evidence is this? I would say there are three minimal requirements for the belief to be sustainable. First, your conscious Ego should evidently be an *immaterial* entity not tied to the body, so that it could, in principle, survive your bodily death. Second, it should evidently be capable of leading an *independent* life, so that it could, in principle, have a future history as "you." Third, it should evidently have endless *staying power*.

We have said enough in previous chapters to show that *immateriality* is never going to be a problem. It is at the very root of what phenomenal consciousness seems to be about. Nearly two hundred years ago the Enlightenment philosopher Sir William Hamilton introduced the term "natural dualists": "I would be inclined to denominate those who implicitly acquiesce in the primitive duality as given in Consciousness, the Natural Dualists. . . . [They] establish the existence of the two worlds of mind and matter on the immediate knowledge we possess of both series of phenomena."[31] Hamilton was not thinking as an evolutionist. But in the last twenty years there has been an increasing realization among psychologists and anthropologists that it is indeed human nature to think this way.[32]

Thus, developmental psychologist Paul Bloom aptly describes human beings as "natural-born dualists."[33] Anthropologist Alfred Gell writes: "It seems that ordinary human beings are 'natural dualists,' inclined more or less from day one, to believe in some kind of 'ghost in the machine' and to attribute the behaviour of social others to the mental representations these others have 'in their heads.'"[34] Neuropsychologist Paul Broks writes: "The separateness of body and mind is a primordial intuition. It has sprung from our evolution as social beings and coalesced into the hardware of the central nervous system. Human beings are natural born soul makers, adept at extracting unobservable minds from the behaviour of observable bodies, including their own."[35] And this, moreover, comes from scholars who have yet to take on board the new ideas about phenomenal consciousness that we have been discussing in this book. As you will realize, all my arguments about the magical mystery show would fall flat if human beings were *not* dualists. It would mean the show had failed.

The first requirement, therefore, is easily met. However, if the conscious Ego is to go on to be immortal, it is not enough that it should simply be immaterial; it must also be *independent* of the material body. And this does not follow necessarily. Suppose, as some have suggested, that consciousness were simply an "epiphenomenon" of neural activity—the mere whistle that accompanies the working of the engine. Then, even though completely immaterial, there would be no reason to think consciousness capable of independent existence.

So, what further evidence might you rely on to prove that the conscious Ego can indeed have a life of its own? The nineteenth-century social anthropologist Edward Tylor suggested the answer is likely to be your firsthand experience of *sleep* and *dreaming*. In his view, dreams seem to provide as good evidence as anyone could ask for that the soul can say good-bye to the body and continue its individual life. While your body sleeps, *engages in no actions,* and *receives no stimulation,* your dream Ego goes its own way, engaging in dramatic adventures of doing and feeling. I would agree with Tylor; there could hardly be a more promising indication that your soul will be able to have a *future life,* even if and when your body is no longer simply dormant but turned to dust.

Independence of the body, however, will still not be enough for immortality. The third requirement is that your soul must have unprecedented *staying power*—indeed, it must be able to endure as *your soul* for ever and ever. But this is certainly asking a great deal. Look around you, and you'll realize that almost nothing on Earth is capable of retaining its identity forever. Change and decay are in everything you see. What, then, other than wishful thinking, could possibly suggest that your own soul might have the miraculous capacity to go on indefinitely?

I believe the answer again lies with the evidence of sleep. I noted earlier one of the most obvious and reliable properties of sleep, which is that in your experience—and by the time you are seventy years old this may be based on twenty-five thousand exemplars—you *always wake up and come to.* But there is something more than a little remarkable about this phenomenon of "coming to." When you fall asleep, your body enters a state of slumber, but it nonetheless remains ticking over, its life continues, ready to resume where it left off. Your consciousness, however, *vanishes completely*. In no sense does it remain ticking over. *You*, as we say, *pass out*. And when you emerge again, either in a dream or when you finally resume waking life, you *emerge from nothing*—but as the very same *you* you were before.

The fact of your self bootstrapping itself back into existence is such a familiar happening that you may not be as astonished by it as you should be. Nonetheless, you can scarcely fail to notice what goes on. And it could well provide an essential plank in your reasoning about immortality. For such a proven capacity for endless *resurrection* out of nothing is of course the one thing that really could guarantee everlasting existence—or at any rate re-existence—for your individual Ego.[36]

Pulling these strands together, we can see that human beings have, to say the least, a good enough set of *excuses* for believing in an afterlife. But I would put it more strongly. I think that unless and until extraneous arguments come into play (most insidiously the arguments of modern natural science), they have good enough *reasons* for believing. Human beings rationally ought to believe in an afterlife. No wonder, then, that almost everyone in the world does believe in it, in one way or another, making it in effect a species-wide human trait.

This is not to say that the belief is simply a "natural intuition," at which everyone arrives spontaneously without cultural input. No doubt children, who are struggling to understand their metaphysical situation, need to think about the issues carefully and will be more than willing to listen to what others have to say. There is evidence that beliefs in an afterlife grow stronger and more specific as children come under the sway of ideas about ghosts, angels, heaven, hell, or whatever the local culture offers. But to suggest, as some anthropologists have done, that because the beliefs are culturally conditioned, and not uniform or universal, they owe relatively little to the evolved properties of the conscious mind cannot be right.[37]

Think again about psychological zombies. We can presume those zombies would never come to believe in their personal survival after death, no matter what they were taught in Sunday school. But then, of course, if I am right, the zombies would do just fine without the belief, because, as I remarked in chapter 6, they would not fear death and the loss of meaning in the first place.

■ Perhaps this seems almost too neat. I have ended up suggesting that consciousness, which—because of its very success in giving individual lives a purpose—was in danger of condemning its human hosts to a prison of anxieties about death, came up in the nick of time with a get-out-of-jail-free card. I agree this would seem to have been an extraordinarily lucky break. Yet *neat things happen*. That is the story of evolution (and if neat things did not happen, it is arguable we would not be here *to see* they did not happen). In any case, nothing in evolution by natural selection is really just a matter of luck (even if luck comes into it).

Throughout this book I have been asking, in relation to each of the public effects of consciousness that I have identified: is it *adaptive*? Is natural selection helping to maintain it as a designed-in feature? And now, with belief in the immortality of the soul, I should ask the same again. True, it may be getting increasingly difficult to untangle low-level biological benefits from higher-level cultural ones. Indeed, it may not make much sense to try to do so. Ideas about immortality have by now become woven so deep into the warp of human societies that even those few individuals who profess not to believe in an afterlife (in the contemporary United States this is still fewer than one in five) may benefit from the positive energy generated by a belief that runs throughout the culture.

Still, we can ask the question. And since, generally, the best way to discover whether a trait is contributing to biological fitness is to investigate what happens when the expression of the trait is blocked, perhaps the question we should really be asking is this: what would the consequences be *if the belief in personal immortality were to be taken away*—taken, that is, from people who already have it and may be coping quite well with their anxieties just because of it?

Now, you might think this can be no more than a thought experiment, because in real life there is no way an experimenter could rob an individual person of his or her unverifiable beliefs about the afterlife (even if they should be so wicked as to want to). But actually this is not entirely true. For there is indeed one experimenter who can do the robbing, and this is the *individual himself.* The individual can entertain *his own doubts.* He can *imagine* that his own belief is false.

You will not need any convincing that such self-doubt is quite common. In fact, it probably happens to almost all humans at some point in their lives that they find themselves imagining the afterlife is a mirage. And there is no shortage of testimony from people who have been to the brink and reported back. I will quote just one example, but a particularly telling one because the doubts were sown by a best friend.

Elizabeth Barrett writes in a letter to her future husband, Robert Browning, in the year of their marriage, 1846:

> Miss Bayley told me ... that she was a materialist of the strictest order, & believed in no soul & no future state. In the face of these conclusions, she said, she was calm & resigned. It is more than I could be, as I confessed. My whole nature would cry aloud against that most pitiful result of the struggle here—a wrestling only for the dust, & not for the crown. What resistless melancholy would fall upon me if I had such thoughts!—& what a dreadful indifference. All grief, to have itself to end in!—all joy, to be based upon nothingness!—all love, to feel eternal separation under & over it! Dreary & ghastly, it would be! I should not have the strength to love you, I think, if I had such a miserable creed. And for life itself, ... would it be worth holding on those terms,—with our blind Ideals making mocks and mows at us wherever we turned? A game to throw up this life would be, as not worth playing to an end![38]

We could hardly have more eloquent proof of how belief in the afterlife can be essential to a person's willingness to continue with her mission here on Earth. Barrett's letter shouts biological adaptiveness—life and love and family all hang in the balance. But let's note how this is working in terms of her psychology, because it is actually quite subtle. Her belief that her soul is immortal makes her bodily life worth living just because the soul, whose life it is, is not destined for extinction. Thus the prospect of life after death gives meaning to life before death and provides her with the all-important *reasons to live* that the prospect of personal oblivion would have undermined. It is true that on one level she will now have *less* of an incentive to fight for life, because she will have less cause to fear death. But this will be more than made up for by the value that has been added to life as such.[39]

It is complicated. But I think we should not be shy of drawing the evolutionary conclusion. If belief in the afterlife really does increase biological fitness, there will have been selection for whatever psychic structures help sustain it. This will have meant selection for phenomenal consciousness and the conscious self as such. But incidentally, it will have meant selection for the ancillary sources of evidence that help to persuade people of the soul's immortality—especially, if I am right, the propensity to dream.

Many nonhuman animals probably have dream experiences of some kind. But experimental psychologists have generally concluded that humans are unique in having *narrative* dreams: dreams in which the individual Ego is at the center of a lifelike story taking place away from the dreamer's physical location.[40] Such dreams, in humans, may well have several biological functions. But encouraging people to believe in the independence of the soul could be a particularly important one.

Given all this, and how much the spiritual health of future generations of our species could depend on it, you may wonder, as I do: is people's belief in the afterlife secure? I suggested above that the one thing that might potentially undermine the belief would be modern science. Miss Bayley's materialist arguments against the existence of an immortal soul were clearly not sufficiently cogent to force Elizabeth Barrett to change her mind. But the day may come—even come soon—

when science will have revealed the illusion of consciousness for what it is, and any rational person will have no choice but to accept the game is up.

What then? Paul Bloom has thought about the possibility and is none too sanguine. When asked by the Edge Question Centre in 2007, "What is your dangerous idea?" he came out with this: "The dangerous idea is that . . . if what you mean by 'soul' is something immaterial and immortal, something that exists independently of the brain, then souls do not exist. . . . The widespread rejection of the soul would . . . require people to rethink what happens when they die, and give up the idea (held by about 90% of Americans) that their souls will survive the death of their bodies and ascend to heaven. It is hard to get more dangerous than that."[41]

I am with him on this. Yet, to look on the brighter (or arguably darker) side, I would point out that some illusions are so well structured that they are effectively immune to invasion by the scientific truth. Look at Richard Gregory's Gregundrum from a position where its true shape is revealed (figure 2 of the opening chapter) and then look back at it from the one position from which it appears impossible (figure 1), and you will still always see the wonderful impossibility rather than the boring truth. So it is, I expect, with consciousness. Every newborn human child, starting over, is bound to see the magical properties of qualia the way Nature intended. And even if a materialist explanation such as mine should win the day with scientists, people's knowledge of this explanation is never going to change the way they experience consciousness first-hand, nor stop them from continuing to build monuments to the human spirit on that foundation. Belief in the immortal soul surely has a lot further to run.

Envoi

Tom Nagel, in "What Is It Like to Be a Bat?" wrote: "Without consciousness the mind-body problem would be much less interesting. With consciousness it seems hopeless."[1] In light of the psychological effects of consciousness we have been considering, let me put it another way: Without consciousness human beings would be much less interesting. With consciousness they seem to be almost too interesting for words.

Nagel continued: "The most important and characteristic feature of conscious mental phenomena is very poorly understood. Most reductionist theories do not even try to explain it. And careful examination will show that no currently available concept of reduction is applicable to it. Perhaps a new theoretical form can be devised for the purpose, but such a solution, if it exists, lies in the distant intellectual future."

The year 2011 hardly counts as the distant future. But we have seen in part 1 of this book how we can already claim some success in the search for a reductionist theory of what phenomenal consciousness *is*—it is a magic show that you stage for yourself inside your own head. In part 2 we have seen how the evidence of natural history provides several good leads as to what consciousness *does*—it lights up the world and makes you personally feel special and transcendent. And now in part 3 we have seen how, in the case of human beings, when individuals reflect on their own situation, this paves the way for spirituality—so that humans reap the rewards, and anxieties, of living in the soul niche. To cap this, we have seen how, in the last stages of this extraordinary story, nature and culture have connived to persuade humans that their souls may be able to live on after bodily death—so that their earthly lives acquire new meaning. Thus, in the end, one of the strengths of this reductionist theory is that it can explain how the experience of being conscious adds to people's lives by convincing them that any reductionist theory must be false.

We have argued that all this is based on a contrived illusion: the sensory ipsundrum, which, as an evolutionary development of sentition, has been designed to appear to the subject to have surreal phenomenal properties. Consciousness is *an impossible fiction*, or, perhaps better said, *a fiction of the impossible*. Yet, the fact is this fiction has worked wonders to improve its subjects' lives. The psychological attitudes that flow from it have been immensely empowering. As William James wrote about a more recent, but related, development, religion, "Every sort of energy and endurance, of courage and capacity for handling life's evils, is set free in those who have religious faith. For this reason, the strenuous type of character will on the battlefield of human history always outwear the easy-going type, and religion will drive irreligion to the wall."[2]

You may think I have left it late in the book to mention religion. And you may ask why at this point I do not make more of it. The reason for my reticence is not that I think religion has been unimportant in human affairs, but rather that religion—at any rate, theistic religion—has not been evolutionarily important. Long before religion could begin to get a foothold in human culture, human beings must already have been living in soul land. Indeed, according to the anthropologist Maurice Bloch, humans had first to invent the "transcendental social," and "religion simply appears as an aspect of this that cannot stand alone."[3] Religion is parasitic on spirituality (and not, as some religionists would have it, the other way round).

It is true that several evolutionary psychologists have wanted to argue that religious belief is a biological adaptation in its own right, some even claiming that there is a genetically constructed "god-module" in the human brain. But I do not find this fits with the evidence—either for the belief in God being sufficiently ancient or for it adding to the chances of *individual survival*.[4] By contrast, the case for consciousness-driven spirituality's being adaptive rests on evidence of a much longer history and of much greater relevance to individual success in life. In fact, I might argue (but at this late stage I won't) that spirituality is probably all the more adaptive *without* religion, because religious belief—especially belief in God—can be something of a drag on it.[5]

I am nearly ready to wrap up. But these last few chapters have been all about *human* consciousness, and an evolutionary theory cannot of course be concerned with one species only. So, we still have questions to answer about how human consciousness relates to that of other creatures, past and present.

I make no apology for the fact that the discussion of the last six chapters *has* been concerned largely with humans. It is not just species chauvinism on my part. Any objective observer—such as our Andromedan visitor—looking at the wider natural history of consciousness across the animal kingdom, could not fail to remark that human consciousness is in a league of its own. In several obvious respects consciousness *matters* more to humans than to any other animal. It plays a bigger and more complex part in shaping their lives and relationships. In fact, humans now provide the best advertisement for consciousness imaginable.

This being so, I think we can safely assume that consciousness has been under *greater pressure from natural selection* in humans than in nonhumans. We might expect therefore that humans have evolved to be more conscious than any other species—that consciousness is more salient, closer to the front of their minds. However, should we also assume that consciousness has been under special kinds of selection pressure in humans? And, if it has been, should we expect humans to have evolved to be not just *more* but *differently conscious*—so that "what it is like" for a human to experience sensations is qualitatively different from what it is like for any other species?

At the end of chapter 6, I first raised the possibility of there being evolved differences in phenomenal quality in relation to our discussion of the fact that human beings, alone among animals, fear their own death. It was, I wrote, a tantalizing question whether this would have meant that human consciousness has been pulled in a novel direction that would have reshaped the ipsundrum. Now, in the chapters since, we have explored other areas where the human penchant for reflecting on the meaning of consciousness might again have exposed the ipsundrum to new evolutionary forces. So we have further reasons for asking that tantalizing question. It is time to answer it, as best we can.

There would seem to be two possible scenarios.

On one hand, it could be that phenomenal consciousness, having evolved under the influence of other factors, such as a simple love of life and the value of having a substantial core self, reached a plateau long before human beings and intellectual reflection came on the scene. In that case the quality of consciousness would already have been something of a fixture—and today it would still remain much the same wherever consciousness exists on Earth. Although consciousness would be contributing to human survival in ways it never did in other animals—and although this could have brought about changes in the way humans access consciousness, as, for example, when they dream—no modifications in the basic quality would have been called for.

On the other hand, it could be that the new uses to which humans were putting consciousness really did create opportunities for doing the job still better by "improving" the quality of phenomenal experience as such: specifically, so as to ramp up the fear of oblivion, to increase the sense of awe, to emphasize loneliness and individuality, to encourage thoughts about immortality, and so on. In that case the ipsundrum might have been remodeled repeatedly in the later stages of human evolution, so that now there are several peculiarly human dimensions to "what it is like."

Who knows how far this might have gone? I think we should at least allow the possibility that humans have evolved to have radically different (and—arguably—radically more wonderful) forms of phenomenal experience than anyone else. I confess I find this possibility as worrying as it is intriguing. One of the comforts for humans of living in the soul niche has been that, once you recognize that other people are as conscious as you are and that you share the same phenomenal world, it is easy and natural to suppose the same holds true for many nonhuman animals. But if this is not so, the curtain of existential separateness begins to close around you again. Does your dog not enjoy being tickled the way you imagine it? Does the skylark miss out on the glories of his own song? Worrying or not, I do not know of any good reason to discount it. I have mentioned already that there may even be anatomical grounds for supposing that sensations in human beings have features that do not exist in other animals.

Nevertheless—call me lacking in courage, if you will—I am inclined to think the truth lies in between. That is, while conscious experience is almost certainly richer, more impressive, and more poignant for humans than for our animal cousins—more truly soul-hammering, to revert to that useful phrase—it still makes use of the same basic tricks. So, the qualities of phenomenal consciousness, which were established early on, are still recognizably the same across all extant conscious species (or would be recognizably the same to the Andromedan scientist if she could—as we earthling scientists cannot yet do—make the comparison). Although the differ-

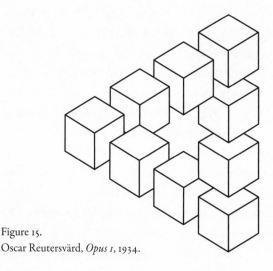

Figure 15.
Oscar Reutersvärd, *Opus 1*, 1934.

ences between humans and nonhumans are there, they are not so great as to make human attempts to imagine what it is like to be an animal completely off target.

Let me explain my view on this further by returning to my favorite metaphor, although I must ask you again not to take it too literally. The impossible triangle, which I called the Penrose triangle in chapter 1, was discovered by the Swedish artist Oscar Reutersvärd in 1934, when, at the age of eighteen, he was doodling in the margin of a textbook during a Latin class. He started by drawing a perfect six-pointed star and then began to add cubes, placing them around the star nestled into the spaces between the points. As he worked on the drawing, he realized he had chanced on a remarkable new kind of object (figure 15).[6]

This was to be the first of many impossible objects that Reutersvärd would go on to create. But the evolution and elaboration of these objects did not happen right away. In

fact, it was not until the 1950s, when Roger Penrose independently came up with same design, that Reutersvärd realized
that the "perspectival deceit" he had hit on with the triangle
could be used to generate a whole family of similarly paradoxical figures. He went on to produce the first "impossible staircase" and the first "Devil's tuning-fork." And soon the ideas
were taken up and embellished by others, most notably by the
Dutch artist M. C. Escher and the Swiss Sandro Del Prete.
Thus it came about that in the next decade Reutersvärd's original drawing spawned more and more complex cathedrals of
impossibility.[7] Figure 16 shows one of the later variants, Del
Prete's *Gateway to the Fourth Dimension* (note how the god-
dess holds the original triangle in her left hand).[8]

Figure 16.
Sandro Del Prete,
Gateway to the
Fourth Dimension,
1966. Copyright
estate of Sandro Del
Prete, reproduced by
permission.

Envoi

So I like to think of there having been a similar evolutionary progression with the ipsundrum. The crucial first step would have been Nature's discovery—through some "natural doodle"—of a variation in the expressive response to sensory stimulation, sentition, that just chanced to steer the reverberatory activity in the feedback loops into a new kind of attractor state: a state that perhaps gave rise to the illusion of existing in "thick time" and so lifted sensation onto the phenomenal plane.

In the nature of things, this innovative step must have occurred at a particular date in a particular evolutionary line (although it is possible it was repeated later in other lines.) Pushing it as far back as seems credible, let me suggest it took place around 300 million years ago in the primitive reptiles that were ancestral to birds and mammals. We can assume that, to have been selected at that time, the innovation would have had to have brought immediate benefits to survival. So let's suppose these would have involved benefits of the kind we discussed in chapters 6 and 7—although no doubt relatively modest versions of them to begin with. Thus, those ancient conscious reptiles would already have been beginning to enjoy the benefits of *having a core self* and of *being there* in an *enchanted world*.

From this point on, any backsliding to the state of having nonphenomenal sensations would have been severely punished by natural selection. Nonetheless, there could have been a long period of stability in which, except for small adjustments and refinements, the ipsundrum underwent no further development. Like other ancient biological inventions, such as the heart, for example, consciousness had reached a plateau of efficiency beyond which no improvements were required.

Envoi

So what consciousness *was like* for those ancient reptiles continued to be what consciousness *is like*; and what its *evolutionary function was* continued to be what its *function is*—for all species of conscious animals that were later descended from them, from crows to cats to dolphins.

All except *one*. With the emergence of human beings, there came into existence a species whose members reflected on their experience in quite new ways. Humans emerged as *connoisseurs of consciousness* who took an unprecedented interest in the phenomenological details of what it is like to be there and pondered its metaphysical ramifications. So, aspects of phenomenal quality became important that would not have counted for anything before. This could have been the cue for major changes in the presentation of sensations, even a complete revamping of the magic show to satisfy this more philosophically demanding audience. Yet, as it happened, I believe this was unnecessary. There was already quite enough "unused" potential in the existing qualities of consciousness for the new demands to be met without departing radically from the original tradition. All it required—and brought about—was some clever restaging: new lighting, a more daring set, additional mirrors to add new layers to the illusion, but still essentially more of the same. Phenomenal consciousness was, in this respect, preadapted to take on its expanded role in humans.

■ As scientists, how could we possibly know? Let me repeat the methodological truth that I emphasized in the first chapter. All we can see as natural historians of consciousness are the behavioral consequences, and these do not necessarily have a unique mapping onto the internal mental states that elicit them. To revert to an earlier analogy, the same smile could be elicited by many different jokes.

In the end there could be only one way to tell, and that must be to go inside the subject's head—armed with the right neurophenomenological laws for translating between brain activity and conscious representations. We have supposed that the Andromedan scientist already has all the necessary tools, so that *she,* unlike us as of now, should be able to compare consciousness across species and individuals and come up with definite answers. Her book *Coming-to Explained,* when she completes it, may even contain a detailed taxonomic guide describing what it is like (or mostly not like) to be any of the animal species here on Earth.

You and I may have a certain feeling of sour grapes about this. It hardly seems fair that an alien scientist should be able to arrive at answers to questions that so deeply interest us about *our* world but that for the foreseeable future we cannot get to for ourselves. But philosophers of science, at least, will be reassured by the knowledge that there is somebody somewhere who is able to answer these questions empirically— which means, if nothing else, that the questions do count as proper scientific questions.

However, I have an admission to make. I do not believe the Andromedan will ever make the visit.

When I introduced her, I wrote: "As a scientist, she has much to look forward to." I wrote this because I assumed her to be a scientist like one of us: one of Poincaré's savants "who studies nature because he takes delight in it, and who takes delight in it because it is beautiful," or one who, like Dawkins, bothers to get up in the mornings because he has "opened his eyes on a sumptuous planet, sparkling with colour, bountiful with life."

But the Andromedan—as I stipulated as a condition of involving her to start with—*is not phenomenally conscious herself*. I noted that this would not stop her from having an exceptionally brilliant analytic mind. Yet the fact remains *she herself is a psychological zombie*. And—as we have learned since—such zombies do not care about things the way that conscious creatures do. In particular they do not see it as their job to be "in love with the universe." I imagined our visitor to be thrilled to watch the dawn rise on Earth and to witness the awakening of conscious minds. But now I am afraid she will have stayed in bed.

It means it is all going to take a bit longer. One of us humans will have to write the book instead.

Envoi

Acknowledgments

I presented an early version of this book as the John Damien Lecture at the University of Stirling, Scotland, in 2007, and since then have test run the ideas at meetings in Oxford, Cambridge, London, Newcastle, Belfast, Genoa, and Kyoto. I am grateful to all those in the audiences whose questions and challenges to what I was saying helped me say it better next time. In 2008 Daniel Dennett hosted a seminar, aboard his sailboat *Xanthippe*, to give me feedback from himself and graduate students, and we spent three happy days tossing ideas around off the coast of Maine. A number of friends have read the book in draft, and their notes have been invaluable. I want to thank especially Ross Anderson, Ruth Brandon, Dylan Evans, Ayla Humphrey, Petter Johansson, Justin Junge, Arien Mack, Anthony Marcel, Natika Newton, Matt Ridley, Rupert Sheldrake, and John Skoyles. It has been my privilege to be represented by the literary agent

John Brockman, whose enthusiasm for the big questions is unbounded. The finished book owes much to my editors, Nick Johnston and Richard Milner at Quercus and Rob Tempio at Princeton University Press, who have been supportive and creative at every stage, and especially to my copyeditor at Princeton, Dalia Geffen.

Acknowledgments

Notes

Invitation

1. See reviews at http://www.humphrey.org.uk/nick_007.htm.

2. Walter Mischel, Editorial, *APS Observer* (September 2008).

3. Bill Rowe, "The Innocent Illusion," *American Journal of Psychology* 121 (2008): 506–13.

4. Steven Poole, *Guardian,* 29 May 2006.

Chapter 1 Coming-to Explained

1. Colin McGinn, "Consciousness and Cosmology: Hyperdualism Ventilated," in *Consciousness*, ed. M. Davies and G. W. Humphrey (Oxford: Blackwell, 1993), pp. 155–77.

2. Jerry Fodor, "Headaches Have Themselves," *London Review of Books,* 24 May 2007, p. 9.

3. Richard Gregory has confirmed: "I think I was the first to make the wooden model Penrose Triangle. It doesn't have a name. What would be a good name? I rather like Gregundrum!" E-mail from Gregory, 16 May 2008.

4. Arthur Conan Doyle, *The Sign of Four* (1890; repr., Harmondsworth: Penguin Classics, 2001), ch. 6, p. 42.

5. The trope of the Andromedan, aka Martian, scientist has been used before. I discussed what a Martian could figure out about consciousness

in Humphrey, "Thinking about Feeling," in *Oxford Companion to the Mind,* ed. R. L.Gregory (Oxford: Oxford University Press, 2004), pp. 213–14. Daniel Dennett took up the same theme still more effectively in "A Third-Person Approach to Consciousness," in *Sweet Dreams* (Cambridge MA: MIT Press, 2005), pp. 25–56. Dennett and I have batted these ideas around for so long now that neither of us can be sure who came first.

6. Jeffrey Gray, "The Contents of Consciousness: A Neuropsychological Conjecture," *Behavioral and Brain Sciences* 18 (1995): 659–722, p. 660.

7. Owen Flanagan, *Consciousness Reconsidered* (Cambridge, MA: MIT Press, 1993), p. 5 (italics are in the original in this and all other quotations).

8. John Searle, *The Rediscovery of the Mind* (Cambridge, MA: MIT Press, 1992), p. 71.

9. David Chalmers, comp., "Zombies on the Web," http://consc.net/zombies.html.

10. On this point, I disagree with the philosopher to whom I am otherwise closest, Daniel Dennett, who has argued that what he calls "heterophenomenology"—the method of looking at everything that shows up in behavior—should be sufficient to reveal all there is to know. See Dennett, *Consciousness Explained* (New York: Little Brown, 1991).

11. Dan Lloyd, *Radiant Cool* (Cambridge, MA: Bradford Books, 2003), p. 16.

12. Mike Beaton provides a sophisticated discussion of the logical problems of explaining qualia. He makes the important point that when arguing from one conceptual level to another, scientific explanation goes *one way* only. Thus, while we can deduce the properties of water from its chemical composition, we cannot deduce the chemical composition from the properties of water. And the same will presumably be true of qualia and the brain: brain states to qualia, yes; qualia to brain states, no. It follows that no one should expect to be able to deduce what happens at the level of his or her brain purely by introspection. Beaton, "Qualia and Introspection," *Journal of Consciousness Studies* 16 (2009): 88–110.

13. John Searle, "The Mystery of Consciousness," pt. 2, *New York Review of Books*, 16 November 1995.

14. I am not dismissing entirely the valiant efforts of the "phenom-

Notes to Chapter 1

218

enologist" philosophers and psychologists, such as Husserl and Merleau-Ponty, to provide a full description of sensory experience. It is just that I don't think they had much success.

15. Nicholas Humphrey, *Seeing Red: A Study in Consciousness* (Cambridge, MA: Harvard University Press, 2006).

16. Consider, as a parallel example here on Earth, how the theory of complex numbers was developed as a mathematical exercise long before it came into use in applied physics.

17. The poet and physician David Sahner, in an essay comparing the ideas of this book to the philosophy of Wallace Stevens, expands on how *poetry* can capture the ineffable: "At their core, qualia and, by extension, integrated phenomenal experiences in general, defy 'verbatim' description. We are left, for example, with anemic terms such as the 'redness of red.' What the poet avails himself of in his efforts to duplicate the felt nuances of experience is poetic technique, consisting mainly of tropes (e.g., symbol, simile and, as Stevens called it in one poem, 'evading metaphor'). Other technical devices that enable poetic legerdemain, with the result that conscious experience is enlarged and made novel, include anthimeria (e.g., use of a noun as a verb), synesthesia (i.e., descriptions of one type of sensation in the parlance of another sense modality), parataxis (the use of a dearth of linking terms, which conveys a rushing effect), and strategies that evoke religious or trance-like feelings through the use of repetition (e.g., anaphora). And this is not all. Line configuration (which may be enjambed to provide double-meaning, tension and even a sense of violence) and rhythm (which may provide intensity, speed, a balm-like effect, or a sense of awkwardness) are carefully deployed by poets. These devices push the envelope of poetic description in a bid to more closely mimic the manner in which experience is actually sensed, in the blaze of all of its affect and meaning-laden intensity." David Sahner, "Phenomenal Experience as a Basis for Selfhood in the Poetry of Wallace Stevens: Communion with a New Theory," manuscript under submission, 2010.

18. Colin McGinn, "Can We Solve the Mind-Body Problem?" *Mind* 98 (1989): 349–66.

Chapter 2 Being "Like Something"

1. René Descartes, *Meditations on First Philosophy*, trans. John Cottingham, Second Meditation (1641; repr., Cambridge: Cambridge University Press, 1986), p. 16.

2. The term "hard problem of consciousness," coined by David Chalmers, refers to the problem of explaining why we have qualitative phenomenal experiences. It is contrasted with the "easy problem" of explaining purely functional abilities—to perceive, discriminate, integrate information, report mental states, focus attention, etc. The easy problem is easy because all that is required for its solution is to specify a computational mechanism that can perform the function. According to Chalmers, hard problems are distinct from this set because they "persist even when the performance of all the relevant functions is explained" (Chalmers, "Facing Up to the Problem of Consciousness," *Journal of Consciousness Studies* 2 [1995]: 200–219).

3. Thomas Nagel, "What Is It Like to Be a Bat?" *Philosophical Review* 83 (1974): 435–50.

4. I will adopt this convention from now on, with "you" being the test case for whatever experience we are discussing, the generic example of a subject. I will use "we" and "I" for us as the discussants.

5. Bridget Riley, "Colour for the Painter," in *Colour: Art and Science*, ed. Trevor Lamb and Janine Bourriau, pp. 31–64 (Cambridge: Cambridge University Press, 1995), p. 31.

6. Natika Newton, "Emergence and the Uniqueness of Consciousness," *Journal of Consciousness Studies* 8 (2001): 47–59, p. 48.

7. Koran 42:11. See the fascinating list of attempts to translate this passage at http://www.islam-muslims.org/Quran/42/11/default.htm.

8. At this point I should acknowledge my further debt to Daniel Dennett, who has stolidly—solidly and brilliantly—maintained that consciousness may indeed be a kind of fiction. See especially Dennett's reply to Eric Schwitzgebel in Dennett, "Heterophenomenology Reconsidered," *Phenonom Cogn Sci* 6 (2007): 247–70.

9. Of course, not everyone will choose so rationally. Sometimes when people are confronted by evidence of events that cannot be accommodated within the known world of physics, they do choose the magical or paranormal interpretation instead. The mathematician John Taylor, for example, was all too ready to throw away his physics books when he

first witnessed Uri Geller's spoon bending (John Taylor, *Superminds: An Enquiry into the Paranormal* [London: Macmillan, 1975]).

10. Wassily Kandinsky, *Concerning the Spiritual in Art*, trans. M.T.H. Sadler (1911; repr., New York: Dover, 1977), p. 25.

11. Dennett, *Consciousness Explained*, p. 107.

12. Bernard Baars has stoutly defended the metaphor of a "theater of consciousness" (although with a different emphasis from me), in, for example, Baars, "In the Theatre of Consciousness: Global Workspace Theory; A Rigorous Scientific Theory of Consciousness," *Journal of Consciousness Studies* 4 (1997): 292–309.

Chapter 3 Sentition

1. The question for all theories, as Thomas Bayes insisted, is not just whether the theory does the job, but how likely it is to be true a priori. Consider, for example, the theory that God made the universe in 4004 BC, complete with all its geological strata, fossils, etc., which can certainly explain the data but is completely implausible on other grounds.

2. You don't think so? Well don't hold me to this. But this is the way I think we could go about giving a robot red qualia. First we would arrange for the robot to make some kind of fancy response to red light falling on its light sensors, while at the same time it keeps track of what it is doing and computes an internal representation of it. To begin with, presumably, the robot will not be especially impressed by this representation of its own response—interesting maybe, but certainly not magical. But we would then fiddle with the design of the response, tweaking it this way and that, with the goal that at some point the robot will suddenly see it in quite a new way. If we are successful, then bingo! The robot will start to claim its experience is soul hammering. And who would we be to deny it?

3. For example, Daniel Dennett, *Kinds of Minds: Towards an Understanding of Consciousness* (New York: Basic Books, 1997); Eva Jablonka and Marion J. Lamb, "The Evolution of Information in the Major Transitions," *Journal of Theoretical Biology* 239 (2006): 236–46; and Derek Denton, *The Primordial Emotions: The Dawning of Consciousness* (Oxford: Oxford University Press, 2005).

4. This is a summary of ideas developed at greater length in Nicholas Humphrey, *A History of the Mind* (New York: Basic Books, 1992); "The

Privatization of Sensation," in *The Evolution of Cognition,* ed. L. Huber and C. Heyes, pp. 241–52 (Cambridge, MA: MIT Press, 2000); and especially *Seeing Red.*

5. Recent evidence on the sensitivity of plants is discussed in Carol Kaesuk Yoon, "Study Hints Plants Have Sensibilities," *New York Times News Service,* 19 June 2008, http://legacy.signonsandiego.com/union-trib/20080619/news_1c19plants.html. The possibility that this might involve some kind of brain is rejected by Amedeo Alpi and thirty-five others; "Plant Neurobiology: No Brain, No Gain?" *Trends in Plant Science* (2008): 12.

6. I must mention here Philip Steadman's suggestion that a camera obscura could be built with a "photographic plate" consisting of cress seeds. The cress would grow only where the light fell on the plate (Steadman, personal communication, October 2008).

7. These are some of the striking homologies between sensation and bodily expression: (1) Ownership. Sensations always *belong to the subject.* When, for example, you experience a red sensation in your visual field or a pain in your toe, you *own* the sensation; it is yours and no one else's; you are the one and only *author* of it. . . . As, for example, when you smile, you *own and are the author of* the smile. (2) Bodily location. Sensations are always *indexical* and invoke a particular part of the subject's body. You feel the red sensation in *this part of your visual field,* you feel the pain in *this part of your foot.* . . . As, when you smile with your lips, the smiling intrinsically involves *this part of your face.* (3) Presentness. Sensations are always in the *present tense, ongoing, and imperfect.* When you experience the red sensation or feel the pain, the sensation is here just now for the time being. The experience did not exist before and will not exist after you stop feeling it. . . . As, when you smile, the smiling too exists just *now.* (4) Qualitative modality. Sensations always have the feel of one of several *qualitatively distinct modalities.* When you have the red sensation, it belongs to the class of *visual* sensations; but when you have the pain, it belongs to the wholly different class of *somatic* sensations. Each modality, linked to its own class of sense organ, has, as it were, its own distinct phenomenal style. . . . As, when you smile with your lips, this expression belongs to the class of facial expressions, as contrasted with, say, vocal expressions or lachrymatory ones. Each expressive modality, linked to its own class of effector organ, has its distinct style of expression. (5) Phenomenal immediacy. Most

important, sensation for the subject is always *phenomenally immediate*, and the four properties just described are *self-disclosing*. Thus, when you have the red sensation, your impression is simply that "I'm doing this, now, in this part of my visual field of my eyes"—and the fact that it is *your* eyes (rather than someone else's), that it is this place in your *eyes* (rather than some other place in your body), that it is happening *now* (rather than some other time), and that it is something occurring in a *visual* way (rather than, say, in an auditory or olfactory way) are facts of which you are directly and immediately aware for the very reason that it is *you, the author of the red sensation, who makes these facts*. So, too, when you smile with your lips, your impression is simply that your lips are smiling, and all the corresponding properties of this action are facts of which you, *the author of the smile*, are immediately aware for similar reasons. (Taken from Humphrey, *Seeing Red*, pp. 82–83.)

Chapter 4 Looping the Loop

1. Francis Crick and Christof Koch, "A Framework for Consciousness," *Nature Neuroscience* 6 (2003): 119–26, p. 119.

2. The figure is taken from http://www.mgix.com/snippets /?MackeyGlass.

3. It was a conversation with the physicist Paul Gailey that first alerted me to the potential of DDEs for explaining qualia.

4. Aristotle *De anima* 3.2.426b, quoted by Daniel Heller-Roazen, *The Inner Touch: Archaeology of a Sensation* (New York: Zone Books, 2007), pp. 54–55.

5. Douglas Hofstadter, *Gödel, Escher, Bach: An Eternal Golden Braid* (New York: Basic Books, 1979).

6. Douglas Hofstadter, *I Am a Strange Loop* (New York: Basic Books, 2007), p. 102.

7. Try Googling the "Shepard-Risset glissando."

8. Steve Jones, in *The Third Culture*, ed. John Brockman (New York: Simon and Schuster, 1996), p. 207.

Chapter 5 So What?

1. Chalmers, "Zombies on the Web."

2. Psychological zombies—who completely lack phenomenal experience—do not exist in practice. But there are human patients with brain damage who are in a state of partial "zombiedom." The best-known ex-

ample is the syndrome of blindsight, where, after damage to the visual cortex, patients are able to see without experiencing visual sensations (I discuss this at more length in Humphrey, *Seeing Red*). Note that the Andromedan scientist, as we have imagined her, is a psychological zombie (not, of course, a philosophical one).

3. Jerry Fodor, "You Can't Argue with a Novel," *London Review of Books,* 3 March 2004, p. 31.

4. Coleridge had what he called a golden rule for dealing with the arguments of other writers with whom he disagreed. Do not presume to say the argument is wrong unless you can see just how the writer came to hold his mistaken views; in other words, until "you understand his ignorance." Samuel Taylor Coleridge, *Biographia Literaria* (New York: Leavitt, Lord, 1834), ch. 12, p. 140.

5. See, for example, Christof Koch: "What benefit for the survival of the organism flows from consciousness? One answer that I hope for is that intelligence, the ability to assess situations never previously encountered and to rapidly come to an appropriate response, requires integrated information." "A Theory of Consciousness," *Scientific American Mind,* 16–19 July 2009, p. 19.

6. Thomas S. Kuhn, *The Structure of Scientific Revolutions* (Chicago: University of Chicago Press, 1970), p. 111.

7. Daniel Dennett, *Sweet Dreams* (Cambridge, MA: MIT Press, 2005), p. 26.

8. Todd M. Preuss and Ghislaine Q. Coleman, "Human Specific Organization of Primary Visual Cortex," *Cerebral Cortex* 12 (2002): 672–91, p. 687.

Chapter 6 Being There

1. Lord Byron to Annabella Milbanke (later Lady Byron), 1813, quoted by Benjamin Woolley, *The Bride of Science: Romance, Reason and Byron's Daughter* (London: Macmillan, 1999), p. 28.

2. Thomas Nagel, *Mortal Questions* (Cambridge: Cambridge University Press, 1979), p. 2.

3. John Galsworthy, *The Silver Spoon* (London: Heinemann, 1926), p. 65.

4. Not to be confused with "presentism" as a technical term in the philosophy of physics.

5. John Keats to C. W. Dilke, 22 September 1819, in *The Life and Letters of John Keats,* ed. Lord Houghton (London: J. M. Dent & Sons), p. 179.

6. Albert Camus, "Nuptials at Tipasa," in *Lyrical and Critical Essays,* ed. Philip Thody, trans. Ellen Conroy Kennedy (1938; repr., New York: Vintage, 1970), p. 65.

7. Rupert Brooke, "The Great Lover," in *1914 and Other Poems* (London: Sidgwick & Jackson, 1915).

8. Allan Fallow, "Gombe's New Generation," *National Geographic Magazine Online Extra,* 2003, http://ngm.nationalgeographic.com/ngm/0304/feature4/online_extra.html.

9. Marc Bekoff, "Are You Feeling What I'm Feeling?" *New Scientist,* 26 May 2007, p. 44.

10. George B. Schaller, *The Last Panda* (Chicago: University of Chicago Press, 1993), p. 66.

11. Report in *New Scientist,* 29 October 1994, p. 108.

12. A. A. Milne, "Spring Morning," in *When We Were Very Young* (London: Methuen, 1924), p. 34.

13. Nicholas Humphrey, field notes, Camp Visoke, Rwanda, 12 May 1971.

14. Aristotle *De sensu et sensibilibus* 7.448a–448b, quoted by Heller-Roazen, *The Inner Touch,* p. 59.

15. Paul Valéry, "Cantiques spirituels," in *Variété: Œuvres,* vol. 1 (1924; repr., Paris: Pléiade, 1957), p. 450.

16. Milan Kundera, *Immortality,* trans. Peter Kussi (London: Faber & Faber, 1991), p. 225.

17. Gottlob Frege, "The Thought: A Logical Inquiry," in *Philosophical Logic,* ed. P. F. Strawson (1918; repr., Oxford: Oxford University Press, 1967), p. 27. (I have replaced the word "experient" in the quotation with the more familiar word "experiencer.")

18. Johann Gottlieb Fichte, *The Science of Knowledge,* ed. and trans. p. Heath and J. Lachs (1794–1802; repr., Cambridge: Cambridge University Press, 1982), p. 97.

19. Marcel Proust, *Swann's Way,* vol. 1 of *Remembrance of Things Past,* trans. C. K. Scott Moncrieff and T. Kilmartin (1913; repr., London: Chatto & Windus), p. 5.

20. Paul Valéry, *Cahiers,* vol. 2 (1974), quoted by Heller-Roazen, *The Inner Touch,* p. 76.

21. Charles Sherrington, *The Integrative Action of the Nervous System* (Cambridge: Cambridge University Press, 1947), p. xviii.

22. Thomas Metzinger, response to a "Talk with Nicholas Humphrey," *Edge,* online edition 144, 5 August 2005 (http://www.edge.org/documents/archive/edge144.html). For a fuller statement, see Metzinger, *The Ego Tunnel: The Science of the Mind and the Myth of the Self* (New York: Basic Books, 2009).

23. James Branch Cabell, *Beyond Life: Dizain des Démiurges* (New York: Robert McBride, 1919), p. 353.

24. William James, *Principles of Psychology*, vol. 1 (New York: Henry Holt, 1890), p. 319.

25. Nagel, *Mortal Questions*, p. 9.

26. Philip Roth, "It No Longer Feels a Great Injustice That I Have to Die," interview by Martin Krasnik, *Guardian,* 14 December 2005, section G2, p. 14.

27. John Dryden, "Translation of the Latter Part of the Third Book of Lucretius: Against the Fear of Death," in *Dryden: Selected Poems* (1685; repr., Harmondsworth: Penguin Classics, 2001).

28. Jesse Bering, "Never Say Die: Why We Can't Imagine Death," *Scientific American Mind*, 22 October 2008, p. 34.

29. Philip Larkin, "Aubade," *Times Literary Supplement*, 23 December 1977.

30. Ernest Becker, *The Denial of Death* (New York: Free Press, 1973), p. xvii.

31. Jean-Jacques Rousseau, *Julie, or The New Eloise*, quoted in D. J. Enright, ed., *The Oxford Book of Death* (1761; repr., Oxford: Oxford University Press, 1983), p. 22.

32. Joe Simpson, *Touching the Void* (London: Jonathan Cape, 1988), p. 109.

33. William Shakespeare, *Measure for Measure*, 3.1.129.

34. Dylan Thomas, "Do Not Go Gentle into That Good Night," in *Dylan Thomas: Selected Poems* (London: J. M. Dent & Sons, 1974), p. 131.

35. Samuel Johnson, quoted by James Boswell, *The Life of Samuel Johnson* (1791; repr., London: Wordsworth, 2008), p. 600.

36. Whether any nonhuman animals have a general capacity for mental time travel remains undecided. But there is persuasive evidence that under special conditions, both chimpanzees and members of the crow

family can in fact plan for the future. See, for example, Mathias Osvath, "Spontaneous Planning for Future Stone Throwing by a Male Chimpanzee," *Current Biology* 19, no. 5 (2009): R190–R191. For a more skeptical view, see Thomas Suddendorf and Michael Corballis, "The Evolution of Foresight: What Is Mental Time Travel, and Is It Unique to Humans?" *Behavioral and Brain Sciences* (2007): 30, 299–313.

37. W. H. Auden and Christopher Isherwood, chorus, *The Dog beneath the Skin* (London: Faber & Faber, 1935).

38. Voltaire, quoted in Enright, *Oxford Book of Death,* p. ix.

39. This is an edited version of Tetsuro Matsuzawa's field notes, which can be found online at http://www.greenpassage.org/green-corridor/education/JokroPamphlet.pdf. For the downloadable video, go to http://www.pri.kyoto-u.ac.jp/chimp/Bossou/Jokro.html. See also Dora Biro et al., "Chimpanzee Mothers at Bossou, Guinea, Carry the Mummified Remains of Their Dead Infants," *Current Biology* 20, no. 8 (2010): R351–R352.

Chapter 7   The Enchanted World

1. Bridget Riley, *Bridget Riley: Dialogues on Art*, ed. Robert Kudielka (London: Zwemmer, 1995), pp. 79–80.

2. Paul Cézanne, quoted by Joachim Gasquet, *Cézanne: A Memoir with Conversations* (London: Thames & Hudson, 1991), p. 162.

3. Walter Pater, *The School of Giorgione*, Studies in the History of the Renaissance (London: Macmillan, 1877), p. 138.

4. William Shakespeare, *Much Ado about Nothing*, 2.3.62.

5. Gerard Manley Hopkins, "Pied Beauty," in *Poems, 1918* (London: Humphrey Milford, 1918).

6. Oscar Hammerstein II, *The Sound of Music* (1965).

7. As I noted in chapter 3, when you look at the red object, you not only have the *sensation* of being stimulated by red light, you also have the *perception* that there is a red object out there. Sensation, as a representation of "what is happening to me," and perception, as a representation of "what is happening out there," have psychologically different functions and are performed by neural pathways that are largely independent of each other (see Humphrey, *Seeing Red*). However, as the eighteenth-century philosopher Thomas Reid observed: "The perception and its corresponding sensation are produced at the same time. In our experience

we never find them disjoined. Hence, we are led to consider them as one thing, to give them one name, and to confound their different attributes. It becomes very difficult to separate them in thought, to attend to each by itself, and to attribute nothing to it which belongs to the other" (Thomas Reid, *Essays on the Intellectual Powers of Man,* pt. 2 [1785; repr., Cambridge, MA: MIT Press, 1969], ch. 17, p. 265).

8. K. Carrie Armel and V. S. Ramachandran, "Projecting Sensations to External Objects: Evidence from Skin Conductance Response," *Proceedings Royal Society Lond. B.* 270 (2003): 1499–1506. Figure 11 reprinted by permission.

9. In *Seeing Red*, I misdescribed one aspect of this. I wrote that "the subject reports feeling pain" when the Band-Aid is ripped off. I regret the exaggeration of saying he actually feels it rather than expects it.

10. The finding was not completely without precedent. In 1996 a case study appeared of a man with Tourette's syndrome, for whom "the itchy sensations preceding motor tics could arise in other people or in objects. The extracorporeal sensations are associated with the need to scratch or touch the itchy item in a particular way. External sensations most frequently arise in angles, corners, and points of objects such as elbows, the edges of tables, or the edge of his computer screen. . . . When younger, the patient would act on the accompanying urge and would scratch his sister's elbow." B. I. Karp and M. Hallett, "Extracorporeal 'Phantom' Tics in Tourette's Syndrome," *Neurology* 46 (1996): 38–40.

11. If the visual-tactile parallels seem somewhat forced, I would point out that vision and touch do in fact share an evolutionary ancestry. "When photoreceptors evolved they were not an entirely new kind of receptor. . . . By packing a sensory cilium with photo-sensitive pigment, it could be made to be specifically excitable by light. Even the rods and cones in the retinas of our own eyes show evidence of having started out this way in evolution—as cilia that were sensitive primarily to touch" (Nicholas Humphrey, *A History of the Mind* [London: Chatto & Windus, 1992], p. 53).

12. Reid, *Essays on the Intellectual Powers,* ch. 16, p. 242.

13. Aldous Huxley, *The Doors of Perception* (New York: Harper and Row, 1954), p. 19.

14. Marcel Proust, *The Captive,* vol. 3 of *Remembrance of Things Past,* trans. C. K. Scott Moncrieff and T. Kilmartin (1923; repr., London: Chatto & Windus, 1981), p. 184.

Notes to Chapter 7

15. William Rothenstein, *Men and Memories* (London: Faber & Faber, 1931), p. 325.

16. Vincent van Gogh to Theo van Gogh, 17 and 27 September 1888, "Van Gogh's Letters: Unabridged and Annotated," at http://www.web exhibits.org/vangogh.

17. Created by G. J. Sawyer and Viktor Deak; text by Esteban Sarmiento, G. J. Sawyer, and Richard Milner, with contributions by Donald C. Johanson, Meave Leakey, and Ian Tattersall, *The Last Human: A Guide to Twenty-two Species of Extinct Humans* (New Haven: Yale University Press, 2007).

18. Marten Shariff, S. Psarakos, and D. J. White, "Ring Bubbles of Dolphins," *Scientific American* 275, no. 2 (1996): 82–87. See also Don White, "Mystery of the Silver Rings," http://www.earthtrust.org/delrings.html.

19. William James, *Varieties of Religious Experience* (New York: Longmans, 1902), p. 137.

20. Robert Louis Stevenson, "Happy Thought," in *A Child's Garden of Verses* (London: Chatto & Windus, 1911).

21. George Santayana, *The Life of Reason*, vol. 1 (New York: Dover, 1905), ch. 10.

22. Rupert Brooke to F. H. Keeling, 20–23 September 1910, quoted by Christopher Hassall, *Rupert Brooke: A Biography* (London: Faber & Faber, 1964), pp. 236–38.

23. Milne, "Spring Morning."

24. Alison Gopnik, Andrew Meltzoff, and Patricia Kuhl, *The Scientist in the Crib* (New York: William Morrow, 1999), p. 85.

25. Richard Dawkins, *Unweaving the Rainbow* (Harmondsworth: Penguin Books, 1998), p. 6.

26. Henri Poincaré, *Science et méthode* (Paris: Flammarion, 1908), p. 22 (my translation).

Chapter 8 So That Is Who I Am!

1. As I write, Alison Gopnik has come out with a new book, *The Philosophical Baby: What Children's Minds Tell Us about Truth, Love and the Meaning of Life* (London: Bodley Head, 2009).

2. John Locke, *An Essay Concerning Human Understanding,* ed. p. Nidditch, bk. 2 (1690; repr., Oxford: Clarendon Press, 1975), ch. 32, sec. 15.

3. When I suggested to the philosopher David Rosenthal that the problem of "the inverted spectrum" was one that every intelligent child

discovers for him- or herself, he said he did not believe this for a moment. Until we have research to establish what is actually the case—that elusive natural history of consciousness—I guess it is his call against mine.

4. James, *Principles of Psychology* 1:226.

5. John Lindner, "The Conscious Universe" (1997), physics course online: http://www3.wooster.edu/Physics/lindner/FYS/introduction.html.

6. John La Touche, lyric for "Ballad for Americans" (1939).

7. Charles Sherrington, *Man on His Nature* (Cambridge: Cambridge University Press, 1940), pp. 324–27.

8. Thomas Huxley, "On the Hypothesis That Animals Are Automata, and Its History," *Fortnightly Review* 95 (1874): 555–80. For more recent, but essentially similar, accounts of the feeling of free will, see Daniel Wegner, *The Illusion of Conscious Will* (Cambridge, MA: MIT Press, 2003), and Daniel Dennett, *Freedom Evolves* (Harmondsworth: Penguin, 2004).

9. Katherine Nelson, *Language in Cognitive Development: The Emergence of the Mediated Mind* (Cambridge: Cambridge University Press, 1998), p. 162.

10. A. A. Milne, "In the Dark," in *Now We Are Six*. See G. Miller, "Foreword by a Psychologist," in Ruth Hirsch Weir, *Language in the Crib* (The Hague: Mouton, 1962), pp. 13–17.

11. Proust, *Swann's Way,* p. 460.

12. William Blake, "A Vision of the Last Judgement," Descriptive Catalogue, in *The Complete Writings of William Blake*, ed. Geoffrey Keynes (1810; repr., Oxford: Oxford University Press, 1957), p. 617.

13. Thomas Traherne, *Centuries of Meditation,* Century I.21 (1670; repr., London: Dent, 1908).

14. Oscar Wilde, *De Profundis: The Complete Text*, ed. Vyvyan Holland (1905; repr., New York: Philosophical Library, 1950), p.104.

15. A. N. Whitehead, *Science and the Modern World* (Cambridge: Cambridge University Press, 1926), pp. 68–69.

16. Rainer Maria Rilke, "Duino Elegies: Ninth Elegy," in *Rilke: Selected Poems*, trans. J. B. Leishman (1922; repr., Harmondsworth: Penguin, 1964).

17. Thomas Traherne, *Centuries of Meditation,* Century III.3 (1670; repr., London: Dent, 1908).

Chapter 9 Being Number One

1. Jakob Burckhardt, *The Civilization of the Renaissance in Italy* (1878; repr., Oxford: Oxford University Press, 1981), p. 81.

2. Peter Abbs, quoted by Anthony Storr, in *Solitude* (London: Flamingo, 1988), p. 80.

3. Marilyn Strathern, *The Gender of the Gift: Problems with Women and Problems with Society in Melanesia* (Berkeley: University of California Press, 1988).

4. Desmond Tutu, "Reflections on the Divine," *New Scientist*, 29 April 2006.

5. Douglas Hofstadter, interview, *New Scientist*, 10 March 2007.

6. Friedrich Nietzsche, *The Gay Science,* trans. W. Kaufmann (New York: Vintage Books, 1974), p. 300.

7. For a sustained attempt at deconstructing notions of individuality, see Raymond Martin and John Barresi, *The Rise and Fall of Soul and Self* (New York: Columbia University Press, 2006).

8. Steven J. Heine, *Cultural Psychology* (New York: W. W. Norton, 2008).

9. Sherrington, *Integrative Action,* p. xviii.

10. Galen Strawson, *Selves: An Essay in Revisionary Metaphysics* (New York: Oxford University Press, 2009). Tom Nagel writes in a review: "What is this subject? As presented in experience, it must be a single mental thing. (That does not exclude its also being physical, but phenomenology tells us nothing about that one way or the other.) However complicated the contents of my consciousness at any moment—if I am listening to Schubert, watching the sunset, drinking wine and trying to remember where I put the car keys—all of it is co-present to a single subject. If selves exist in reality, according to Strawson, they must be mental individuals of this kind, for which he coins the unappealing term sesmet—short for 'subject-of-experience-as-single-mental-thing.'" Nagel, "The I in Me," *London Review of Books*, November 2009, pp. 33–34.

11. Clarice Lispector, *Near to the Wild Heart*, trans. Giovanni Pontiero (1944; repr., New York: New Directions Publishing, 1990).

12. Let's be clear that this is *not* a reversion to the idea of a Cartesian Theater. It is more like Bernard Baars's perfectly respectable idea of a "global workspace"; see Baars, *In the Theater of Consciousness: The Workspace of the Mind* (New York: Oxford University Press, 1997).

13. The most dramatic example is multiple personality disorder or, as it has been renamed, dissociative identity disorder. See Nicholas Humphrey and Daniel Dennett, "Speaking for Ourselves: An Assessment of Multiple Personality Disorder," *Raritan* 9 (1989): 68–98.

14. Proust, *Swann's Way*, p. 5.

15. Nicholas Humphrey, "One Self: A Meditation on the Unity of Consciousness," *Social Research* 67, no. 4 (2000): 32–39. For more on the question of an infant's selfhood, see Gopnik, *Philosophical Baby*.

16. A revealing example in the musical sphere is the computer-generated jazz player GenJam, which learns to jam with a human trumpeter, playing four other instruments, until all five come together as a united quintet. Al Biles, its creator and accompanist, writes: "In addition to playing full-chorus improvised solos, GenJam listens to what I play on trumpet and responds interactively when we trade fours or eights. It also engages in collective improvisation, where we both solo simultaneously and GenJam performs a smart echo of my improvisation, delayed by anywhere from a beat to a measure. Finally, it listens to me as I solo and play the 'head' of a tune and breeds my measures with its ideas, which steers its solo on a tune in the direction of what I've just played on that tune" (http://www.it.rit.edu/~jab/GenJam.html).

17. Kundera, *Immortality*, p. 225.

18. What about the so-called extended mind? The philosopher Andy Clark has taken the lead in arguing that we should think of the mind as having a cognitive architecture that extends beyond the brain to include all sorts of add-ons in the external world—including other people. (See Clark, *Supersizing the Mind: Embodiment, Action, and Cognitive Extension* [New York: Oxford University Press, 2009].) Clark himself, however, draws the line at the idea of *extended consciousness*. In a significant new paper he writes: "In this paper I review a variety of arguments for the extended conscious mind, and find them flawed. Arguments for extended cognition, I conclude, do not generalize to arguments for an extended conscious mind." Clark, "Spreading the Joy? Why the Machinery of Consciousness Is (Probably) Still in the Head," *Mind* 118 (2009): 963–93, p. 963.

19. James, *Principles of Psychology* 1:289.

20. Oscar Wilde, *The Picture of Dorian Gray* (London: Bigelow Smith, 1909), p. 185.

21. Oscar Wilde, *An Ideal Husband* (1895; repr., London: Dover, 2000), p. 50.

22. For an early account of the development of theory of mind, see my book *The Inner Eye* (London: Faber & Faber, 1986); for one of the latest, see Gopnik, *Philosophical Baby*.

23. Traherne, *Centuries of Meditation*.

Chapter 10 Entering the Soul Niche

1. Michel Bitbol, lecture at a conference titled "Science and Spirituality," Cortona, Italy, June 2009.

2. James, *Principles of Psychology* 1:180–81.

3. Ibid. The quotations in this and the following paragraph are from pp. 344–47.

4. Keith Ward, *In Defence of the Soul* (Oxford: Oneworld, 1998), p. 142.

5. F. J. Odling-Smee, K. N. Laland, and M. W. Feldman, *Niche Construction: The Neglected Process in Evolution*, Monographs in Population Biology 37 (Princeton: Princeton University Press, 2003).

6. Ian Hacking, "The Looping Effect of Human Kinds," in *Causal Cognition: An Interdisciplinary Approach*, ed. D. Sperber et al. (Oxford: Oxford University Press, 1995), pp. 351–83.

7. Cabell, *Beyond Life*, p. 356.

8. Rock painting at Vilafamés, Valencia, Spain, listed (but not illustrated) as UNESCO World Heritage Site 874-359 (1998), http://whc.unesco .org/en/list/874; height 25 cm. The image here is taken from my photograph, which was then subjected to "contour tracing" by the CorelDraw software program. I am grateful to Xavier Allepuz Marzà, archaeologist of the town hall of Vilafamés, for allowing me access and giving permission to publish this image.

9. Humphrey, "The Privatization of Sensation."

Chapter 11 Dangerous Territory

1. Susanne Langer, *Mind: An Essay on Human Feeling,* vol. 3 (Baltimore: Johns Hopkins University Press, 1982), p. 103.

2. Yevgeny Yevtushenko, "People," in *Selected Poems,* trans. Robin Milner-Gulland and Peter Levi (1961; repr., London: Penguin, 2008), p. 85.

3. Randolph Nesse, "What Good Is Feeling Bad? The Evolutionary Utility of Psychic Pain," *The Sciences* (November/December 1991): 30–37, p. 37.

4. Sophocles, *Antigone,* in *The Theban Plays,* trans. E. Watling (Harmondsworth: Penguin Classics, 1947), p. 136, l. 370.

5. Doctor: Why are you depressed, Alvy?

Alvy's Mom: It's something he read.

Doctor: Something he read, huh?

Alvy at 9: The universe is expanding.

Doctor: The universe is expanding?

Alvy: Well, the universe is everything, and if it's expanding, someday it will break apart and that would be the end of everything!

Alvy's Mom: What is that your business? [*she turns to the doctor*]

Alvy's Mom: He stopped doing his homework!

Alvy: What's the point?

Alvy's Mom: What has the universe got to do with it? You're here in Brooklyn! Brooklyn is not expanding!

Doctor: It won't be expanding for billions of years yet, Alvy. And we've gotta try to enjoy ourselves while we're here!

Woody Allen, *Annie Hall* (1977), http://www.imdb.com/title/tt0075686/quotes.

6. Auden and Isherwood, *The Dog Beneath the Skin.*

7. Nagel, *Mortal Questions,* p. 9.

8. Albert Camus, *The Myth of Sisyphus,* trans. Justin O'Brien (1942; repr., New York: Penguin, 1975), p. 4.

9. Santayana, *The Life of Reason.*

10. David Hume, "The Sceptic," in *Essays: Moral, Political and Literary,* ed. E. F. Miller, pt. 1, essay 18 (1742; repr., New York: Cosimo, 2007), p. 161.

11. Woody Allen, interview with S. Houpt, *Globe and Mail,* 23 April 2002, R-1.

12. George Steiner, *Grammars of Creation* (London: Faber & Faber, 2001), p. 5.

13. C. J. Jung, *The Development of Personality,* trans. R.F.C. Hull (1934; repr., London: Routledge, 1992), p. 169.

14. Gerard Manley Hopkins, "No Worst, There Is None," in *Poems, 1918* (London: Humphrey Milford, 1918).

Notes to Chapter 11

15. Erwin Stengel, *Suicide and Attempted Suicide* (Harmondsworth: Penguin, 1969), p. 37.

16. John Milton (1663), *Paradise Lost*, bk. 10, l. 981.

17. Susan Sontag, *The Volcano Lover* (London: Jonathan Cape, 1992), p. 116.

18. Ludwig Wittgenstein, remark to David Pinsent, quoted in David Edmonds and John Eidinow, *Wittgenstein's Poker* (London: Faber & Faber, 2001), p. 155.

19. Ann F. Garland and Edward Zigler, "Adolescent Suicide Prevention," *American Psychologist* 48 (1993): 169–82.

20. If there were no inbreeding, the number would be 2 to the power 2,000! Of course, in reality many of your ancestors were related, so the number is much smaller.

21. Deut. 30:19.

22. Stanley H. Ambrose, "Late Pleistocene Human Population Bottlenecks, Volcanic Winter, and Differentiation of Modern Humans," *Journal of Human Evolution* 34 (1998): 623–51; W. Amos and J. Hoffman, "Evidence That Two Main Bottleneck Events Shaped Modern Human Genetic Diversity," *Proceedings of the Royal Society, Biological Sciences,* 7 October 2009.

23. Søren Kierkegaard, *The Sickness unto Death,* trans. Alastair Hannay (1849; repr., Harmondsworth: Penguin, 2008) p. 51.

Chapter 12 Cheating Death

1. Milan Kundera, *The Book of Laughter and Forgetting,* trans. Aaron Asher (New York: Viking Penguin, 1980), pp. 206–7.

2. Walter Hagen, *The Walter Hagen Story* (New York: Simon and Schuster, 1956), ch. 32.

3. Blaise Pascal, *Pensées,* trans. A. J. Krailsheimer (1669; repr., Harmondsworth: Penguin, 1966), pp. 48, 95.

4. Frank Ramsey, *The Foundations of Mathematics* (London: Routledge & Kegan Paul, 1931), p. 291.

5. David Hume, *A Treatise of Human Nature*, ed. L. A. Selby-Bigge (1739; repr., Oxford: Oxford University Press, 1978), bk. 1, pt. 4, sec. 7, p. 269.

6. Michel Ferrari, "William James and the Denial of Death," *Journal of Consciousness Studies* 9 (2002): 117–40, p. 134.

7. Albert Camus, "Summer in Algiers," in *Lyrical and Critical Essays*, p. 91.

8. Pascal, *Pensées*, p. 43.

9. BBC 1 TV, 17 September 2003.

10. See http://www.beforeyoudie.co.uk/50-Things-To-Do-Before-You -Die.htm.

11. Bertrand Russell: "There was a footpath leading across fields to New Southgate, and I used to go there alone to watch the sunset and contemplate suicide. I did not, however, commit suicide, because I wished to know more of mathematics." *Autobiography*, vol. 1 (London: Allen & Unwin, 1967), p. 43.

12. Benjamin Errett, "Australians Debate Ethics of Dying Boy's Wish for Sex," *National Post* (Canada), 22 December 2001.

13. Hume, "The Sceptic."

14. "List of Texas Inmates' Last Meals," now deleted from the official Texas Web site but subsequently posted at the Memory Hole: http:// www.thememoryhole.org/deaths/texas-final-meals.htm. Several prisoners requested cigarettes, but these were prohibited because of prison regulations regarding health and safety.

15. A. Lin Neumann, "Death Watch: A Night at the Gas Chamber," *Columbia Journalism Review,* July/August 1992.

16. Samuel Johnson, quoted by Michael Ignatieff, in *The Needs of Strangers* (London: Chatto and Windus, 1984), p. 86.

17. Pascal, *Pensées*, p. 82.

18. Mary Oliver, "When Death Comes," in *New and Selected Poems, 1992* (Boston: Beacon Press, 1992), p. 10.

19. Brooke, "The Great Lover."

20. Steve Watkins and Clare Jones, *Unforgettable Things to Do before You Die* (London: BBC Books, 2005).

21. John Donne, "Holy Sonnet XIII" (1663).

22. Bertrand Russell, *Portraits from Memory and Other Essays* (New York: Simon and Schuster, 1956), p. 52.

23. Peter Berger and Thomas Luckmann, *The Social Construction of Reality: A Treatise in the Sociology of Knowledge* (New York: Anchor Books, 1966), p. 101.

24. J. Greenberg, S. Solomon, and T. Pyszczynski, "Terror Management Theory of Self-Esteem and Cultural World Views: Empirical As-

sessments and Conceptual Refinements," *Advances in Experimental Social Psychology* 29 (1997): 61–139.

25. Jerry Falwell, on *700 Club,* Pat Robertson's radio chat show, 13 September 2001, quoted in *New York Times,* 14 September 2001.

26. For a recent critique of TMT and a robust reply, see C. D. Navarrete and D.M.T. Fessler, "Normative Bias and Adaptive Challenges: A Relational Approach to Coalitional Psychology and a Critique of Terror Management Theory," *Evolutionary Psychology* 3 (2005): 297–325; and M. J. Landau, S. Solomon, T. Pyszczynski, and J. Greenberg, "On the Compatibility of Terror Management Theory and Perspectives on Human Evolution," *Evolutionary Psychology* 5 (2007): 476–519.

27. David Galin, "The Concepts 'Self,' 'Person,' and 'I,' in Western Psychology and in Buddhism," in *Buddhism and Science,* ed. B. Allan Wallace, pp. 107–44 (New York: Columbia University Press, 2003).

28. George Howison, in a letter dated 18 November 1898, quoted in William James, *Essays in Religion and Morality* (Cambridge, MA: Harvard University Press, 1982), p. 183, n. 75.2.

29. Woody Allen, widely attributed but unsourced.

30. Carl Stumpf, letter dated 26 March 1904, quoted in Ralph Barton Perry, *The Thought and Character of William James,* vol. 2 (Westport, CT: Greenwood Press, 1996), p. 342.

31. William Hamilton, *The Metaphysics of Sir William Hamilton, Collected, Arranged, and Abridged by Francis Bowen* (1836; repr., Ann Arbor: University of Michigan Press, 2005), p. 201.

32. I may have been the first to revive the term "natural dualists," in my book *Leaps of Faith* (New York: Basic Books, 1995), but the term has independently achieved a wider currency since then.

33. Paul Bloom, *Descartes' Baby* (New York: Basic Books, 2004).

34. Alfred Gell, *Art and Agency* (Oxford: Clarendon Press, 1998), p. 127.

35. Paul Broks, "Out of Mind," *Prospect,* April 2005, p. 10.

36. Galen Strawson explicitly rejects this view of things, arguing in *Selves* that the self that returns after a gap in consciousness is *not* the same self that disappeared; I don't know about the *actual metaphysics,* but it is good enough for me if you still *think it's the same you.*

37. There has recently been a ding-dong battle between psychologists and anthropologists about the "naturalness" of afterlife beliefs. Jesse Bering has made a strong pitch for the beliefs as an evolved adaptation; see Jesse Bering, "The Folk Psychology of Souls," *Behavioral and Brain Sciences* 25

(2006): 253–498. Rita Astuti and Paul Harris have argued that they are more of a cultural product; see Rita Astuti and Paul L. Harris, "Understanding Mortality and the Life of the Ancestors in Rural Madagascar," *Cognitive Science* 32 (2008): 713–40. I am inclined to think both are true.

38. Elizabeth Barrett to Robert Browning, 7 May 1846, in *The Letters of Robert Browning and Elizabeth Barrett Browning, 1845–1846,* vol. 2 (New York: Harper and Brothers, 1899), p. 136.

39. That afterlife beliefs can in certain circumstances bring on death rather than postpone it is made clear by the rare but apparently genuine cases of individuals who have welcomed death as a doorway to a better life, notably suicide bombers.

40. See my discussion of dreaming in chapter 7 of *The Inner Eye.*

41. Paul Bloom, "The Rejection of Soul," in *What Is Your Dangerous Idea?* ed. John Brockman (New York: Harper Perennial, 2007), pp. 4–5.

Envoi

1. Thomas Nagel, "What Is It Like to Be a Bat?", p. 435.

2. William James, *Essays in Pragmatism* (1970; repr., New York: Hafner, 1948), p. 86.

3. Maurice Bloch, "Why Religion Is Nothing Special but Is Central," *Philosophical Transactions B.* 363 (2008): 2055–61.

4. Religions, to begin with, will certainly not have involved belief in a supernatural God. Suppose we tentatively date the creation of the soul niche to the time of the Upper Paleolithic revolution, fifty thousand years ago. There is evidence of ritualized burial, cave painting, music, and shamanism, all following soon after, but there is no evidence whatever for a belief in God until about six thousand years ago.

5. The best scientific appraisal of the functions of religion is by Robert A. Hinde, *Why Gods Persist*, 2nd ed. (Abingdon: Routledge, 2010).

6. See http://im-possible.info/english/art/reutersvard/sketch01.html.

7. Reutersvärd's priority as the inventor was celebrated in 1982 with a series of Swedish postage stamps.

8. This version of Sandro Del Prete's drawing (there are several) is at http://im-possible.info/english/art/delprete/delprete1.html.

Index

Index

Index

soul niche: as adaptive environment, 159; defined, 158; human construction of, 159
Sound of Music, 108
Steadman, Philip, 222n.6
Steiner, George, 172
Stevenson, Robert Louis, 120
strange loop, 61
Strathern, Marylyn, 141
Strawson, Galen, 143, 231n10, 237n.36
Stumpf, Carl, 193
subjective present. *See* "thick time"
suicide, 169, 173; bombers, 238n.39
symbolic immortality, 188, 191

terror management theory, 188
"thick time," 21, 60- 62, 90, 211; and strange loop, 62
Things to Do before You Die (BBC book), 180, 185
Thomas, Dylan, 98
Touching the Void, 97
Traherne, Thomas, 134, 138, 152
Tutu, Desmond, 152

Tylor, Edward, 196

Valéry, Paul, 90, 91
van Gogh, Vincent, 118
Vilafamés, 163
visual cortex, 78
Voltaire, 99

Ward, Keith, 158
Whitehead, Alfred North, 135
Wilde, Oscar: on self-love, 150; on sensations, 135
will to live, 86
Wittgenstein, Ludwig, 27, 174
World Trade Center, 9/11, 190

zombie, philosophical: defined, 11; impossibility of, 13, 17, 70
zombie, psychological: Andromedan scientist as, 214, 223n.2; defined, 70; failings of, 70, 88–89, 96, 109, 120, 198; human horror of being, 80; nonhuman animal as, 76